Beginning Serverless Computing

Developing with Amazon Web Services, Microsoft Azure, and Google Cloud

Maddie Stigler

Apress®

Beginning Serverless Computing

Maddie Stigler
Richmond, Virginia, USA

ISBN-13 (pbk): 978-1-4842-3083-1   ISBN-13 (electronic): 978-1-4842-3084-8
https://doi.org/10.1007/978-1-4842-3084-8

Library of Congress Control Number: 2017961537

Cover image designed by Freepik

Managing Director: Welmoed Spahr
Editorial Director: Todd Green
Acquisitions Editor: Joan Murray
Development Editor: Laura Berendson
Technical Reviewer: Brandon Atkinson
Coordinating Editor: Jill Balzano
Copy Editor: James A. Compton
Compositor: SPi Global
Indexer: SPi Global
Artist: SPi Global

Distributed to the book trade worldwide by Springer Science+Business Media New York, 233 Spring Street, 6th Floor, New York, NY 10013. Phone 1-800-SPRINGER, fax (201) 348-4505, e-mail orders-ny@springer-sbm.com, or visit www.springeronline.com. Apress Media, LLC is a California LLC and the sole member (owner) is Springer Science + Business Media Finance Inc (SSBM Finance Inc). SSBM Finance Inc is a **Delaware** corporation.

For information on translations, please e-mail rights@apress.com, or visit http://www.apress.com/rights-permissions.

Apress titles may be purchased in bulk for academic, corporate, or promotional use. eBook versions and licenses are also available for most titles. For more information, reference our Print and eBook Bulk Sales web page at http://www.apress.com/bulk-sales.

Any source code or other supplementary material referenced by the author in this book is available to readers on GitHub via the book's product page, located at www.apress.com/9781484230831. For more detailed information, please visit http://www.apress.com/source-code.

Printed on acid-free paper

This is dedicated to my supportive friends and family.

Contents

About the Author

Maddie Stigler is a professional developer for a consulting firm based in Richmond, Virginia. She is a part of the core team for Women Who Code in Richmond and is involved in many local Microsoft and Amazon meetups. Her interest in cloud computing began while studying computer science at the University of Virginia and has only grown since then. Maddie has maintained a fascination with serverless technology from the start and has applied principles of serverless design and architecture both in her professional and personal work, including developing a flight status service for travel insurance customers using AWS Lambda and Node.js. Her favorite application to date has been creating Amazon Alexa skills by utilizing Lambda functions written in Node.js and triggering them with the Alexa Skills Kit. Maddie plans to continue pursuing her interest in growing cloud technologies and serverless architecture and share her knowledge so that others can do the same.

About the Technical Reviewer

Brandon Atkinson is an accomplished technology leader with over 14 years of industry experience encompassing analysis, design, development, and implementation of enterprise-level solutions. His passion is building scalable teams and enterprise architecture that can transform businesses and alleviate pain points. Brandon leads technology projects, helping to shape the vision, providing technical thought leadership, and implementation skills to see any project through. He has extensive experience in various technologies/methodologies including: Azure, AWS, .NET, DevOps, Cloud, JavaScript, Angular, Node.js, and more.

When not building software, Brandon enjoys time with his wife and two girls in Richmond, VA.

CHAPTER 1

■ ■ ■

Understanding Serverless Computing

Serverless architecture encompasses many things, and before jumping into creating serverless applications, it is important to understand exactly what serverless computing is, how it works, and the benefits and use cases for serverless computing. Generally, when people think of serverless computing, they tend to think of applications with back-ends that run on third-party services, also described as code running on ephemeral containers. In my experience, many businesses and people who are new to serverless computing will consider serverless applications to be simply "in the cloud." While most serverless applications are hosted in the cloud, it's a misperception that these applications are entirely serverless. The applications still run on servers that are simply managed by another party. Two of the most popular examples of this are AWS Lambda and Azure functions. We will explore these later with hands-on examples and will also look into Google's Cloud functions.

What Is Serverless Computing?

Serverless computing is a technology, also known as *function as a service (FaaS)*, that gives the cloud provider complete management over the container the functions run on as necessary to serve requests. By doing so, these architectures remove the need for continuously running systems and serve as event-driven computations. The feasibility of creating scalable applications within this architecture is huge. Imagine having the ability to simply write code, upload it, and run it, without having to worry about any of the underlying infrastructure, setup, or environment maintenance... The possibilities are endless, and the speed of development increases rapidly. By utilizing serverless architecture, you can push out fully functional and scalable applications in half the time it takes you to build them from the ground up.

Serverless As an Event-Driven Computation

Event-driven computation is an architecture pattern that emphasizes action in response to or based on the reception of events. This pattern promotes loosely coupled services and ensures that a function executes only when it is triggered. It also encourages developers to think about the types of events and responses a function needs in order to handle these events before programming the function.

© Maddie Stigler 2018
M. Stigler, *Beginning Serverless Computing*, https://doi.org/10.1007/978-1-4842-3084-8_1

In this event-driven architecture, the functions are event consumers because they are expected to come alive when an event occurs and are responsible for processing it. Some examples of events that trigger serverless functions include these:

- API requests

- Object puts and retrievals in object storage

- Changes to database items

- Scheduled events

- Voice commands (for example, Amazon Alexa)

- Bots (such as AWS Lex and Azure LUIS, both natural-language-processing engines)

Figure 1-1 illustrates an example of an event-driven function execution using AWS Lambda and a method request to the API Gateway.

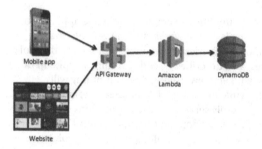

Figure 1-1. *A request is made to the API Gateway, which then triggers the Lambda function for a response*

In this example, a request to the API Gateway is made from a mobile or web application. API Gateway is Amazon's API service that allows you to quickly and easily make RESTful HTTP requests. The API Gateway has the specific Lambda function created to handle this method set as an integration point. The Lambda function is configured to receive events from the API Gateway. When the request is made, the Amazon Lambda function is triggered and executes.

An example use case of this could be a movie database. A user clicks on an actor's name in an application. This click creates a GET request in the API Gateway, which is pre-established to trigger the Lambda function for retrieving a list of movies associated with a particular actor/actress. The Lambda function retrieves this list from DynamoDB and returns it to the application.

Another important point you can see from this example is that the Lambda function is created to handle a single piece of the overall application. Let's say the application also allows users to update the database with new information. In a serverless architecture, you would want to create a separate Lambda function to handle this. The purpose behind this separation is to keep functions specific to a single event. This keeps them lightweight, scalable, and easy to refactor. We will discuss this in more detail in a later section.

Functions as a Service (FaaS)

As mentioned earlier, serverless computing is a cloud computing model in which code is run as a service without the need for the user to maintain or create the underlying infrastructure. This doesn't mean that serverless architecture doesn't require servers, but instead that a third party is managing these servers so they are abstracted away from the user. A good way to think of this is as "Functions as a Service" (FaaS). Custom event-driven code is created by the developer and run on stateless, ephemeral containers created and maintained by a third party.

FaaS is often how serverless technology is described, so it is good to study the concept in a little more detail. You may have also heard about IaaS (infrastructure as a service), PaaS (platform as a service), and SaaS (software as a service) as cloud computing service models.

IaaS provides you with computing infrastructure, physical or virtual machines and other resources like virtual-machine disk image library, block, and file-based storage, firewalls, load balancers, IP addresses, and virtual local area networks. An example of this is an Amazon Elastic Compute Cloud (EC2) instance. PaaS provides you with computing platforms which typically includes the operating system, programming language execution environment, database, and web server. Some examples include AWS Elastic Beanstalk, Azure Web Apps, and Heroku. SaaS provides you with access to application software. The installation and setup are removed from the process and you are left with the application. Some examples of this include Salesforce and Workday.

Uniquely, FaaS entails running back-end code without the task of developing and deploying your own server applications and server systems. All of this is handled by a third-party provider. We will discuss this later in this section.

Figure 1-2 illustrates the key differences between the architectural trends we have discussed.

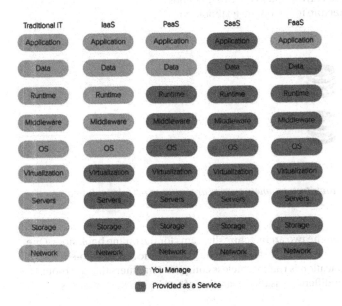

Figure 1-2. *What the developer manages compared to what the provider manages in different architectural systems*

How Does Serverless Computing Work?

We know that serverless computing is event-driven FaaS, but how does it work from the vantage point of a cloud provider? How are servers provisioned, auto-scaled, and located to make FaaS perform? A point of misunderstanding is to think that serverless computing doesn't require servers. This is actually incorrect. Serverless functions still run on servers; the difference is that a third party is managing them instead of the developer. To explain this, we will use an example of a traditional three-tier system with server-side logic and show how it would be different using serverless architecture.

Let's say we have a website where we can search for and purchase textbooks. In a traditional architecture, you might have a client, a load-balanced server, and a database for textbooks.

Figure 1-3 illustrates this traditional architecture for an online textbook store.

Figure 1-3. *The configuration of a traditional architecture in which the server is provisioned and managed by the developer*

In a serverless architecture, several things can change including the server and the database. An example of this change would be creating a cloud-provisioned API and mapping specific method requests to different functions. Instead of having one server, our application now has functions for each piece of functionality and cloud-provisioned servers that are created based on demand. We could have a function for searching for a book, and also a function for purchasing a book. We also might choose to split our database into two separate databases that correspond to the two functions.

Figure 1-4 illustrates a serverless architecture for an online textbook store.

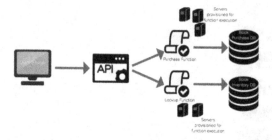

Figure 1-4. *The configuration of a serverless architecture where servers are spun up and down based on demand*

There are a couple of differences between the two architecture diagrams for the online book store. One is that in the on-premises example, you have one server that needs to be load-balanced and auto-scaled by the developer. In the cloud solution, the application is run in stateless compute containers that are brought up and down by triggered functions. Another difference is the separation of services in the serverless example.

How Is It Different?

How is serverless computing different from spinning up servers and building infrastructure from the ground up? We know that the major difference is relying on third-party vendors to maintain your servers, but how does that make a difference in your overall application and development process? The main two differences you are likely to see are in the development of applications and the independent processes that are used to create them.

Development

The development process for serverless applications changes slightly from the way one would develop a system on premises. Aspects of the development environment including IDEs, source control, versioning, and deployment options can all be established by the developer either on premises or with the cloud provider. A preferred method of continuous development includes writing serverless functions using an IDE, such as Visual Studio, Eclipse, and IntelliJ, and deploying it in small pieces to the cloud provider using the cloud provider's command-line interface. If the functions are small enough, they can be developed within the actual cloud provider's portal. We will walk through the uploading process in the later chapters to give you a feel for the difference between development environments as well as the difference in providers. However, most have a limit on function size before requiring a zip upload of the project.

The command-line interface (CLI) is a powerful development tool because it makes serverless functions and their necessary services easily deployable and allows you to continue using the development tools you want to use to write and produce your code. The Serverless Framework tool is another development option that can be installed using NPM, as you will see in greater detail later in the chapter.

Independent Processes

Another way to think of serverless functions is as serverless microservices. Each function serves its own purpose and completes a process independently of other functions. Serverless computing is stateless and event-based, so this is how the functions should be developed as well. For instance, in a traditional architecture with basic API CRUD operations (GET, POST, PUT, DELETE), you might have object-based models with these methods defined on each object. The idea of maintaining modularity still applies in the serverless level. Each function could represent one API method and perform one process. Serverless Framework helps with this, as it enforces smaller functions which will help focus your code and keep it modular.

Functions should be lightweight, scalable, and should serve a single purpose. To help explain why the idea of independent processes is preferred, we will look at different architectural styles and the changes that have been made to them over time. Figure 1-5 illustrates the design of a monolithic architecture.

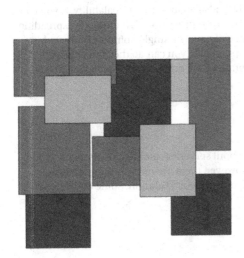

Figure 1-5. *This figure demonstrates the dependency each functionally distinct aspect of the system has on another*

A monolithic application is built as a single interwoven unit with a server-side application that handles all requests and logic associated with the application. There are several concerns with this architecture model. A concern during the development period might be that no developer has a complete understanding of the system, because all of the functionality is packaged into one unit. Some other concerns include inability to scale, limited re-use, and difficulty in repeated deployment.

The microservices approach breaks away from the monolithic architecture pattern by separating services into independent components that are created, deployed, and maintained apart from one another. Figure 1-6 illustrates the microservices architecture.

Figure 1-6. *This figure demonstrates the independent services that make up a microservices architecture*

Many of the concerns that we saw with the monolithic approach are addressed through this solution. Services are built as individual components with a single purpose. This enables the application to be consumed and used by other services more easily and efficiently. It also enables better scalability as you can choose which services to scale up or down without having to scale the entire system. Additionally, spreading functionality across a wide range of services decreases the chance of having a single point of failure within your code. These microservices are also quicker to build and deploy since you can do this independently without building the entire application. This makes the development time quicker and more efficient, and also allows for faster and easier development and testing.

Benefits and Use Cases

One thing many developers and large businesses struggle with about serverless architecture is giving cloud providers complete control over the platform of your service. However, there are many reasons and use cases that make this a good decision that can benefit the overall outcome of a solution. Some of the benefits include these:

- Rapid development and deployment
- Ease of use
- Lower cost
- Enhanced scalability
- No maintenance of infrastructure

Rapid Development and Deployment

Since all of the infrastructure, maintenance, and autoscaling are handled by the cloud provider, the development time is much quicker and deployment easier than before. The developer is responsible only for the application itself, removing the need to plan for time to be spent on server setup. AWS, Azure, and Google also all provide function templates that can be used to create an executable function immediately.

Deployment also becomes a lot simpler, thus making it a faster process. These cloud providers have built-in versioning and aliasing for developers to use to work and deploy in different environments.

Ease of Use

One of the greater benefits in implementing a serverless solution is its ease of use. There is little ramp-up time needed to begin programming for a serverless application. Most of this simplicity is thanks to services, provided by cloud providers, that make it easier to implement complete solutions. The triggers that are necessary to execute your function are easily created and provisioned within the cloud environment, and little maintenance is needed.

Looking at our event-driven example from earlier, the API gateway is completely managed by AWS but is easily created and established as a trigger for the Lambda function in no time. Testing, logging, and versioning are all possibilities with serverless technology and they are all managed by the cloud provider. These built in features and services allow the developer to focus on the code and outcome of the application.

Lower Cost

For serverless solutions, you are charged per execution rather than the existence of the entire applications. This means you are paying for exactly what you're using. Additionally, since the servers of the application are being managed and autoscaled by a cloud provider, they also come at a cheaper price than what you would pay in house. Table 1-1 gives you a breakdown of the cost of serverless solutions across different providers.

Table 1-1. *Prices for Function Executions by Cloud Provider as of Publication*

AWS Lambda	Azure Functions	Google Cloud Functions
First million requests a month free	First million requests a month free	First 2 million requests a month free
$0.20 per million requests afterwards	$0.20 per million requests afterwards	$0.40 per million requests afterwards
$0.00001667 for every GB-second used	$0.000016 for every GB-second used	$0.000025 for every GB-second used

Enhanced Scalability

With serverless solutions, scalability is automatically built-in because the servers are managed by third-party providers. This means the time, money, and analysis usually given to setting up auto-scaling and balancing are wiped away. In addition to scalability, availability is also increased as cloud providers maintain compute capacity across availability zones and regions. This makes your serverless application secure and available as it protects the code from regional failures. Figure 1-7 illustrates the regions and zones for cloud providers.

Figure 1-7. *This figure, from* blog.fugue.co, *demonstrates the widespread availability of serverless functions across cloud providers*

Cloud providers take care of the administration needed for the compute resources. This includes servers, operating systems, patching, logging, monitoring, and automatic scaling and provisioning.

Netflix Case Study with AWS

Netflix, a leader in video streaming services with new technology, went with a serverless architecture to automate the encoding process of media files, the validation of backup completions and instance deployments at scale, and the monitoring of AWS resources used by the organization.

To apply this, Netflix created triggering events to their Lambda functions that synchronized actions in production to the disaster recovery site. They also made improvements in automation with their dashboards and production monitoring. Netflix accomplished this by using the triggering events to prove the configuration was actually applicable.

Limits to Serverless Computing

Like most things, serverless architecture has its limits. As important as it is to recognize when to use serverless computing and how to implement it, it is equally important to realize the drawbacks to implementing serverless solutions and to be able to address these concerns ahead of time. Some of these limits include

- You want control of your infrastructure.

- You're designing for a long-running server application.

- You want to avoid vendor lock-in.

- You are worried about the effect of "cold start."

- You want to implement a shared infrastructure.

- There are a limited number of out-of-the-box tools to test and deploy locally.

We will look at options to address all of these issues shortly. Uniquely, FaaS entails running back-end code without the task of developing and deploying your own server applications and server systems. All of this is handled by a third-party provider.

Control of Infrastructure

A potential limit for going with a serverless architecture is the need to control infrastructure. While cloud providers do maintain control and provisioning of the infrastructure and OS, this does not mean developers lose the ability to determine pieces of the infrastructure.

Within each cloud provider's function portal, users have the ability to choose the runtime, memory, permissions, and timeout. In this way the developer still has control without the maintenance.

Long-Running Server Application

One of the benefits of serverless architectures is that they are built to be fast, scalable, event-driven functions. Therefore, long-running batch operations are not well suited for this architecture. Most cloud providers have a timeout period of five minutes, so any process that takes longer than this allocated time is terminated. The idea is to move away from batch processing and into real-time, quick, responsive functionality.

If there is a need to move away from batch processing and a will to do so, serverless architecture is a good way to accomplish this. Let's take a look at an example. Say we work for a travel insurance company and we have a system that sends a batch of all flights for the day to an application that monitors them and lets the business know when a flight is delayed or cancelled. Figure 1-8 illustrates this application.

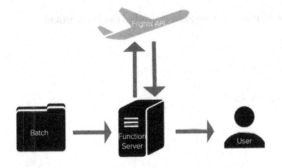

Figure 1-8. *The configuration of a flight monitoring application relying on batch jobs*

To modify this to process and monitor flights in real time, we can implement a serverless solution. Figure 1-9 illustrates the architecture of this solution and how we were able to convert this long-running server application to an event-driven, real-time application.

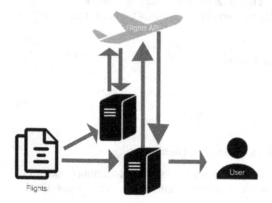

Figure 1-9. *The configuration of a flight monitoring application that uses functions and an API trigger to monitor and update flights*

This real-time solution is preferable for a couple of reasons. One, imagine you receive a flight you want monitored after the batch job of the day has been executed. This flight would be neglected in the monitoring system. Another reason you might want to make this change is to be able to process these flights quicker. At any hour of the day that the batch process could be occurring, a flight could be taking off, therefore also being neglected from the monitoring system. While in this case it makes sense to move from batch to serverless, there are other situations where batch processing is preferred.

Vendor Lock-In

One of the greatest fears with making the move to serverless technology is that of vendor lock-in. This is a common fear with any move to cloud technology. Companies worry that by committing to using Lambda, they are committing to AWS and either will not be able to move to another cloud provider or will not be able to afford another transition to a cloud provider.

While this is understandable, there are many ways to develop applications to make a vendor switch using functions more easily. A popular and preferred strategy is to pull the cloud provider logic out of the handler files so it can easily be switched to another provider. Listing 1-1 illustrates a poor example of abstracting cloud provider logic, provided by serverlessframework.com.

Listing 1-1. A handler file for a function that includes all of the database logic bound to the FaaS provider (AWS in this case)

```
const db = require('db').connect();
const mailer = require('mailer');

module.exports.saveUser = (event, context, callback) => {
 const user = {
  email: event.email,
  created_at: Date.now()
 }
```

```
db.saveUser(user, function (err) {
  if (err) {
    callback(err);
  } else {
    mailer.sendWelcomeEmail(event.email);
    callback();
  }
});
};
```

The code in Listing 1-2 illustrates a better example of abstracting the cloud provider logic, also provided by serverlessframework.com.

Listing 1-2. A handler file that is abstracted away from the FaaS provider logic by creating a separate Users class

```
class Users {
 constructor(db, mailer) {
  this.db = db;
  this.mailer = mailer;
 }

 save(email, callback) {
  const user = {
   email: email,
   created_at: Date.now()
  }

  this.db.saveUser(user, function (err) {
   if (err) {
    callback(err);
   } else {
    this.mailer.sendWelcomeEmail(email);
    callback();
   }
});
 }
}

module.exports = Users;

const db = require('db').connect();
const mailer = require('mailer');
const Users = require('users');

let users = new Users(db, mailer);

module.exports.saveUser = (event, context, callback) => {
 users.save(event.email, callback);
};
```

The second method is preferable both for avoiding vendor lock-in and for testing. Removing the cloud provider logic from the event handler makes the application more flexible and applicable to many providers. It also makes testing easier by allowing you to write traditional unit tests to ensure it is working properly. You can also write integration tests to verify that integrations with other services are working properly.

"Cold Start"

The concern about a "cold start" is that a function takes slightly longer to respond to an event after a period of inactivity. This does tend to happen, but there are ways around the cold start if you need an immediately responsive function. If you know your function will only be triggered periodically, an approach to overcoming the cold start is to establish a scheduler that calls your function to wake it up every so often.

In AWS, this option is CloudWatch. You can set scheduled events to occur every so often so that your function doesn't encounter cold starts. Azure and Google also have this ability with timer triggers. Google does not have a direct scheduler for Cloud functions, but it is possible to make one using App Engine Cron, which triggers a topic with a function subscription. Figure 1-10 illustrates the Google solution for scheduling trigger events.

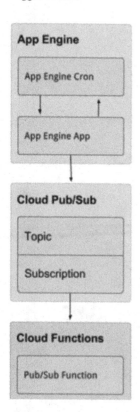

Figure 1-10. *This diagram from Google Cloud demonstrates the configuration of a scheduled trigger event using App engine's Cron, Topic, and Cloud functions*

An important point to note about the cold start problem is that it is actually affected by runtime and memory size. C# and Java have much greater cold start latency than runtimes like Python and Node.js. In addition, memory size increases the cold start linearly (the more memory you're using, the longer it will take to start up). This is important to keep in mind as you set up and configure your serverless functions.

Shared Infrastructure

Because the benefits of serverless architecture rely on the provider's ability to host and maintain the infrastructure and hardware, some of the costs of serverless applications also reside in this service. This can also be a concern from a business perspective, since serverless functions can run alongside one another regardless of business ownership (Netflix could be hosted on the same servers as the future Disney streaming service). Although this doesn't affect the code, it does mean the same availability and scalability will be provided across competitors.

Limited Number of Testing Tools

One of the limitations to the growth of serverless architectures is the limited number of testing and deployment tools. This is anticipated to change as the serverless field grows, and there are already some up-and-coming tools that have helped with deployment. I anticipate that cloud providers will start offering ways to test serverless applications locally as services. Azure has already made some moves in this direction, and AWS has been expanding on this as well. NPM has released a couple of testing tools so you can test locally without deploying to your provider. Some of these tools include node-lambda and aws-lambda-local. One of my current favorite deployment tools is the Serverless Framework deployment tool. It is compatible with AWS, Azure, Google, and IBM. I like it because it makes configuring and deploying your function to your given provider incredibly easy, which also contributes to a more rapid development time.

Serverless Framework, not to be confused with serverless architecture, is an open source application framework that lets you easily build serverless architectures. This framework allows you to deploy auto-scaling, pay-per-execution, event-driven functions to AWS, Azure, Google Cloud, and IBM's OpenWhisk. The benefits to using the Serverless Framework to deploy your work include

- Fast deployment: You can provision and deploy quickly using a few lines of code in the terminal.

- Scalability: You can react to billions of events on Serverless Framework; and you can deploy other cloud services that might interact with your functions (this includes trigger events that are necessary to execute your function).

- Simplicity: The easy-to-manage serverless architecture is contained within one yml file that the framework provides out of the box.

- Collaboration: Code and projects can be managed across teams.

Table 1-2 illustrates the differences between deployment with Serverless Framework and manual deployment.

Table 1-2. *Comparing the configuration of a scheduled trigger event using App engine Cron, Topic, and Cloud functions in a serverless and a manual deployment*

Function	Serverless vs Manual Deployment	
	Serverless Framework	Manual Deployment
Cron	Security out of the box	Security built independently
Topic	Automatic creation of services	Services built independently
Cloud	Reproduction resources created Pre-formatted deployment scripts	Reproduction resources have to be created separately Write custom scripts to deploy function

The figure gives you a good overview of the Serverless Framework and the benefits to using it. We will get some hands-on experience with Serverless later, so let's look into how it works. First, Serverless is installed using NPM (node package manager) in your working directory. NPM unpacks Serverless and creates a `serverless.yml` file in the project folder. This file is where you define your various services (functions), their triggers, configurations, and security. For each cloud provider, when the project is deployed, compressed files of the functions' code are uploaded to object storage. Any extra resources that were defined are added to a template specific to the provider (CloudFormation for AWS, Google Deployment Manager for Google, and Azure Resource Manager for Azure). Each deployment publishes a new version for each of the functions in your service. Figure 1-11 illustrates the serverless deployment for an AWS Lambda function.

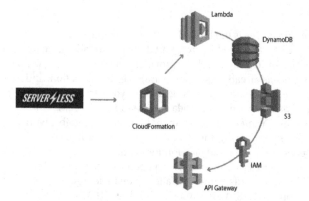

Figure 1-11. *This figure demonstrates how Serverless deploys an application using CloudFormation, which then builds out the rest of the services in the configured project*

Serverless Platform is one of the leading development and testing tools for serverless architecture. As serverless technology progresses, more tools will come to light both within the cloud provider's interfaces and outside.

Conclusion

In this chapter you learned about serverless applications and architecture, the benefits and use cases, and the limits to using the serverless approach. It is important to understand serverless architecture and what it encompasses before designing an application that relies on it. Serverless computing is an event-driven, functions-as-a-service (FaaS) technology that utilizes third-party technology and servers to remove the problem of having to build and maintain infrastructure to create an application. The next chapter will discuss the differences between the three providers we're exploring (AWS, Azure, Google), development options, and how to set up your environment.

CHAPTER 2

■ ■ ■

Getting Started

In order to get started developing serverless applications, we need to look at the serverless offerings and environments for AWS, Azure, and Google, our choices for development platforms and toolkits, and how to set up our environment for them. As discussed in the previous chapter, serverless doesn't mean that no servers are involved, but rather the servers are hosted by different third-party providers. Some of the most prevalent providers for this serverless option include AWS, Azure, and Google. We will examine how the serverless options differ from provider to provider. We will also walk through the environment setup process using Visual Studio Code, Node.js, and Postman.

■ **Note** There are many different development tools, environments, and SDKs that can be used to develop serverless applications. We will go over a couple other options in this chapter and later discuss why we will be using the ones specific to this tutorial.

What Each Provider Offers

Amazon Web Services, Microsoft Azure, and Google Cloud Platform are three of the most prevalent third-party providers for serverless technology. In this chapter, we will discuss the serverless options for each and how they are different from one another. This will give you a better understanding of each offering to help you choose between cloud providers when you write your own serverless applications.

AWS Lambda

Amazon's serverless offering is AWS Lambda. AWS was the first major cloud provider to offer serverless computing, in November 2014. Lambda was initially available only with a Node.js runtime, but now it offers C#, Java 8, and Python. Lambda functions are built independently from other resources but are required to be assigned to an IAM (Identity and Access Management) role. This role includes permissions for CloudWatch, which is AWS's cloud monitoring and logging service. From the Lambda console, you can view various metrics on your function. These metrics are retained within the CloudWatch portal for thirty days. Figure 2-1 illustrates the CloudWatch logging metrics that are available.

© Maddie Stigler 2018
M. Stigler, *Beginning Serverless Computing*, https://doi.org/10.1007/978-1-4842-3084-8_2

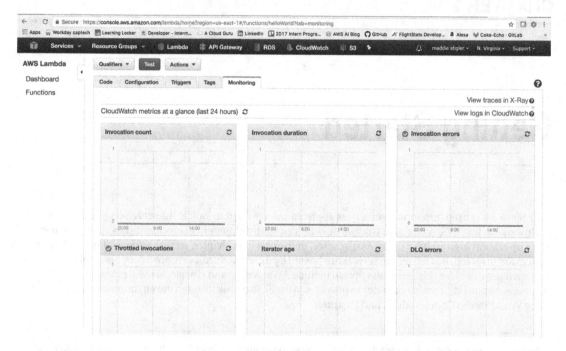

Figure 2-1. *Monitoring logs that are available in CloudWatch. As you can see, for this Hello World function, we don't have any invocations in the past 24 hours. There are even more logging metrics that can be seen from the CloudWatch portal.*

AWS Lambda functions can be written in the AWS console; however, this is not recommended for larger projects. Currently, you cannot see the project structure within the console. You can only see the index.js file, or the function that is handling the event. This makes it difficult to develop within the console. While you can still export the files from the console to view the file structure, you are then back to being limited by the deployment and testing process.

Lambda has built-in Versioning and Aliasing tools that can be utilized straight from the console as well. These tools let you create different versions of your function and alias those versions to different stages. For instance, if you're working with a development, testing, and production environment, you can alias certain versions of your Lambda function to each to keep these environments separate. Figure 2-2 illustrates an example of aliasing a version of your function.

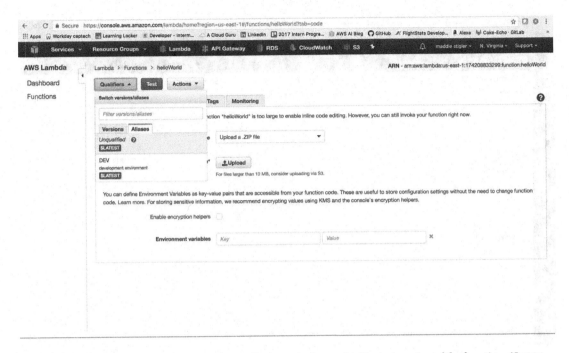

Figure 2-2. *This illustrates a DEV alias that is always pointing at the $Latest version of the function. $Latest simply indicates the most up-to-date version of the Lambda function.*

AWS Lambda also makes it easy to incorporate environment variables. These can be set using a key/value pair, so you can use variables throughout your function to reference protected information such as API keys and secrets, as well as database information. They also give you a better way to pass variables to your function without having to modify your code in several areas. For example, if a key changes, you only need to change it in one spot.

Azure Functions

Microsoft released its serverless offering, Azure Functions, at the Build conference in 2016. Despite being developed only a year and a half after AWS Lambda, Azure Functions remains a strong competitor in the serverless world. Azure Functions supports JavaScript, C#, F#, Python, PHP, Bash, Batch, and PowerShell.

One of Azure's strengths is its ability to integrate Application Insights with your functions. While AWS also has this capability, integrating X-Ray with Lambda, it is important to point out the power of Application Insights. This extensible Application Performance Management tool for developers can be used across many platforms. It uses powerful monitoring tools to help you understand potential performance weaknesses in your application. Figure 2-3 illustrates Application Insights being used for live monitoring of an application.

Figure 2-3. *Live Metrics Streaming monitors incoming requests, outgoing requests, overall health, and servers used to handle requests. You can see how long the requests take and how many requests fail. You can use these statistics to adjust the memory and response of your function.*

Another aspect of Azure functions is that they are built within *resource groups*, containers used to hold all related resources for an Azure solution. It is up to the developer to determine how the resources are grouped and allocated, but it generally makes sense to group the resources of an application that share the same life cycle so they can be deployed, updated, and deleted together. Lambda functions are organized independently. They aren't required to belong to a resource group, but instead can be developed completely separately from any other AWS resources.

One of the potential limitations to serverless functions that we discussed in Chapter 1 was the fear of the "cold start." Azure functions run on top of WebJobs, which means the function files aren't just sitting in a zip file. They are built on top of WebJobs to more easily host long or short back-end processes.

Azure functions are also integrated with several continuous deployment tools, such as Git, Visual Studio Team Services, OneDrive, Dropbox, and Azure's own built-in editor. Visual Studio Team Services (previously Visual Studio Online) is a powerful tool for continuous integration of your functions with a team. The tight integration with Visual Studio Team Services means you can configure the connection to Azure and deploy very easily. It also gives you free Azure function templates out of the box to speed up the development process even further. Currently, this integration is not something that either AWS or Google Cloud provide. It includes Git, free private repos, agile development tools, release management, and continuous integration.

Google Cloud Functions

Google Cloud released its serverless offering, Google Cloud Functions, in February of 2016. Currently, Google Cloud supports only a JavaScript runtime with only three triggers.

■ **Note** It is important to keep in mind that, at this writing, Google Cloud Functions is still in its Beta release. A lot of its functionality and environment is subject to change with more development to its service offering expected.

Google Cloud Functions has automatic logging enabled and written to the Stackdriver Logging tool. The logs remain in Stackdriver for up to thirty days and log real-time insights as well as custom logs. In addition, performance is recorded in Stackdriver Monitoring and the Stackdriver Debugger allows you to debug your code's behavior in production. With Google Cloud Functions you can also use Cloud Source repositories to deploy functions directly from a GitHub or bitbucket repository. This cuts down on time that would be spent manually zipping and uploading code through the console. It also allows you to continue using your form of version control as you would before.

A unique aspect of Google Cloud Functions is its integration with Firebase. Mobile developers can seamlessly integrate the Firebase platform with their functions. Your functions can respond to the following events generated by Firebase:

- Real-time database triggers

- Firebase authentication triggers

- Google Analytics for Firebase triggers

- Cloud storage triggers

- Cloud pub/sub triggers

- HTTP triggers

Cloud Functions minimizes boilerplate code, allowing you to easily integrate Firebase and Google Cloud within your functions. There is also little or no maintenance associated with Firebase. By deploying your code to functions, the maintenance associated with credentials, server configuration, and the provisioning and supply of servers goes away. You can also utilize the Firebase CLI to deploy your code and the Firebase console to view and sort logs.

To be able to run and test your code locally, Google Cloud provides a function emulator. This is a Git repository that allows you to deploy, test, and run your functions on your local machine before deploying it directly to Google Cloud.

A difference between the Google Cloud platform and Azure or AWS is the heavy reliance on APIs for each service. This is similar to the Software Development Kits used in AWS and Azure; however, it is more low-level. Google Cloud relies on API client libraries to obtain service functionality. These APIs allow you to access Google Cloud platform products from your code and to automate your workflow. You can access and enable these APIs through the API Manager Dashboard, shown in Figure 2-4.

Figure 2-4. *The API Manager Dashboard shows all of your currently enabled APIs, along with the requests, errors, latency, and traffic associated with those APIs. The dashboard statistics go back thirty days.*

Explore Triggers and Events

Chapter 1 gave an overview of triggers and events and how they fit into the larger idea of serverless architecture. In this section we will examine what triggers are, how they work with different cloud providers and within real-world examples, and how events drive serverless functions.

What Are Triggers?

Triggers are simply events. They are services and HTTP requests that create events to wake up the functions and initiate a response. Triggers are usually set within the function console or the command-line interface and are typically created within the same cloud provider's environment. A function must have exactly one trigger.

In AWS a trigger can be an HTTP request or an invocation of another AWS service. Azure functions utilize service triggers as well, but they also capture the idea of *bindings*. Input and output bindings offer a declarative way to connect to data from within your code. Bindings are not unlike triggers in that you, as the developer, specify connection strings and other properties in your function configuration. Unlike triggers, bindings are optional and a function can have many bindings. Table 2-1 illustrates the input and output bindings that Azure supports for its functions.

Table 2-1. *Input/Output Bindings for Azure Functions*

Input	Output
	HTTP (REST or Webhook)
Blob Storage	Blob Storage
	Events
	Queues
	Queues and Topics
Storage Tables	Storage Tables
SQL Tables	SQL Tables
NoSQL DB	NoSQL DB
	Push Notifications
	Twilio SMS Text
	SendGrid Email

An example of an application binding a trigger to a function is writing to a table with an API request. Let's say we have a table in Azure storing employee information and whenever a POST request comes in with new employee information, we want to add another row to the table. We can accomplish this using an HTTP trigger, an Azure function, and Table output binding.

By using the trigger and binding, we can write more generic code that doesn't make the function rely on the details of the services it interacts with. Incoming event data from services become input values for our function. Outputting data to another service, such as adding a row to a table in Azure Table Storage, can be accomplished using the return value of our function. The HTTP trigger and binding have a *name* property that works as an identifier to be used in the function code to access the trigger and binding.

The triggers and bindings can be configured in the integrate tab in the Azure Functions portal. This configuration is reflected in the function.json file in the function directory. This file can also be configured manually in the Advanced Editor. Figure 2-5 shows the integration functionality with the input and output settings that can be configured.

Figure 2-5. *The triggers, inputs, and outputs that can be set and configured witin the Azure portal*

The ability to configure outputs using bindings within Azure is something that isn't available with every cloud provider, but having specific outputs based on the reception of trigger events is a concept that is embraced by other cloud providers and one that fits the idea of creating serverless functions to perform single operations.

Triggers within Cloud Providers

Different cloud providers offer different triggers for their functions. While many of them are essentially the same service with a different name based on the provider, some are truly unique. Table 2-2 shows the triggers for the providers we will be using.

Table 2-2. *Function triggers for AWS, Azure, and Google*

AWS Lambda	Azure Functions	Google Cloud Functions
Amazon S3	Azure Storage	
Amazon DynamoDB		
Amazon Kinesis Stream	Azure Event Hubs	
Amazon Simple Notification Service	Queues and Topics	Google Cloud Pub/Sub triggers
Amazon Simple Email Service		
Amazon Cognito		
AWS CloudFormation		
Amazon CloudWatch Logs		
Amazon CloudWatch Events		
AWS CodeCommit		
Scheduled Events	Azure Schedule	
AWS Config		
Amazon Alexa		
Amazon Lex		
Amazon API Gateway	HTTP (REST or WebHook)	HTTP

Development Options, Toolkits, SDKs

In this section, we will look at the various development options, toolkits, and SDKs that can be used to develop serverless applications. Specifically, we will discuss Typescript with Node.js, AWS SDKs, Azure SDK, and the Cloud SDK for Google.

TypeScript with Node.JS

TypeScript is a superset of JavaScript that was developed by Microsoft to develop strongly typed language that compiles to JavaScript. It starts with the same syntax that developers who work with JavaScript know and use today. TypeScript compiles directly to JavaScript code that runs on any browser in many JavaScript engines, including Node.js.

TypeScript enables developers to build JavaScript applications that will also include static checking and code refactoring. Figure 2-6 illustrates an example of compiling TypeScript to JavaScript.

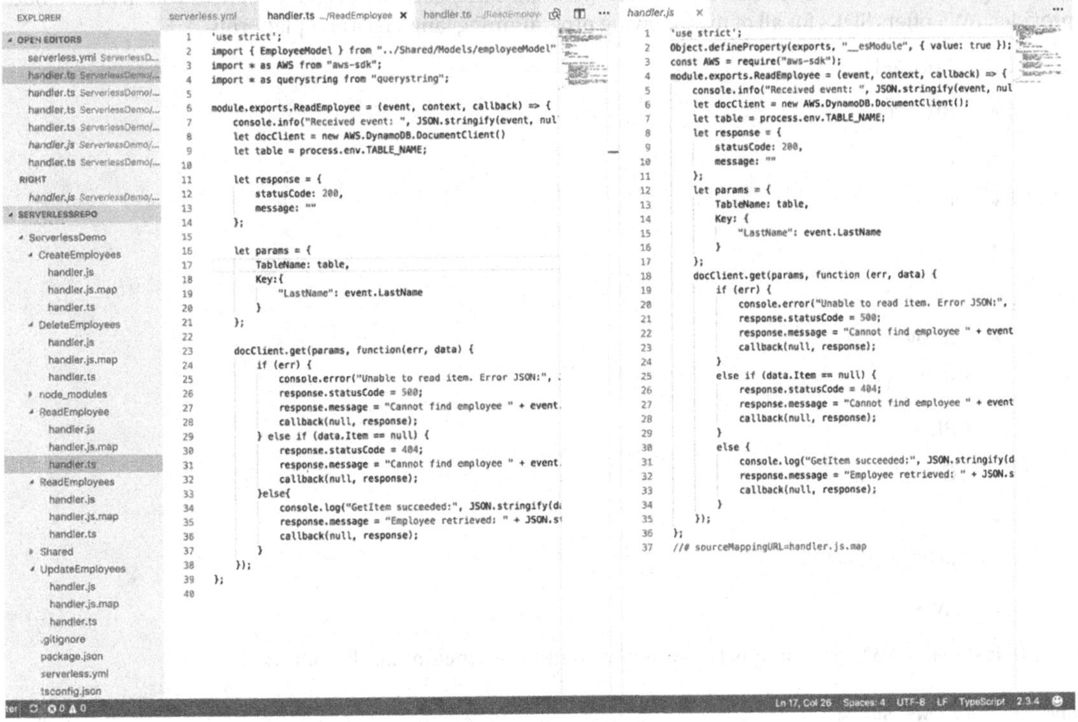

Figure 2-6. *This figure demonstrates the use of TypeScript to create a* Create Employee *function and how it compiles to JavaScript code that can be used to build serverless applications.*

TypeScript can be downloaded using NPM or Visual Studio plug-ins. From the terminal/command prompt, you can install TypeScript with the command `npm install -g typescript`. This gives you access to the TypeScript tools. In Visual Studio, TypeScript is included by default; so I recommend installing Visual Studio Code at this point if needed.

Once TypeScript is installed, you can begin writing TypeScript files and compiling them either using the command line:

```
tsc helloWorld.ts
```

or by building the project in Visual Studio. Once the TypeScript files have compiled, you will see JavaScript files created from the TypeScript files.

AWS SDK

Software development kits (SDKs) are powerful tools for developing serverless applications. AWS, Azure, and Google each have an SDK with which developers can easily access and create services within each cloud provider. AWS offers SDKs for all of the following programming languages and platforms:

- Android
- Browser
- iOS
- Java
- .NET
- Node.js
- Ruby
- Python
- PHP
- Go
- C++
- AWS Mobile
- AWS IoT

To install the AWS SDK, simply type this command at your command prompt:

```
npm install aws-sdk
```

Before you can do this, you will need to have NPM installed. Node Package Manager takes care of the installation for you and makes it accessible in your projects. Figure 2-7 illustrates how the AWS SDK works with Node.js to deliver accessible AWS services to your code.

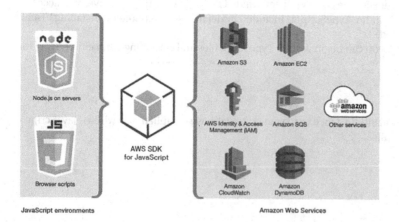

Figure 2-7. *This figure illustrates how the AWS SDK for JavaScript allows you to build full-scale applications that utilize the services that AWS has to offer with little effort*

After installing the SDK, you will need to do some configuration within your Node.js files to load the AWS package into the application. The way to do this is by using the require statement at the top of your JavaScript. The code should look like this:

```
var AWS = require('aws-sdk');
```

You can then access the various AWS resources using the AWS variable you created and the API reference materials that can be found here:

```
https://docs.aws.amazon.com/AWSJavaScriptSDK/latest/index.html
```

This documentation will show you how to create and access particular services. The following example code shows how you can create a table in DynamoDB using the AWS SDK.

```
'use strict';
Object.defineProperty(exports, "__esModule", { value: true });
var AWS = require("aws-sdk");
module.exports.CreateTable = (event, context, callback) => {
  var dynamodb = new AWS.DynamoDB();
  var docClient = new AWS.DynamoDB.DocumentClient();
  var params = {
    TableName: process.env.TABLE_NAME,
    KeySchema: [
      { AttributeName: "LastName", KeyType: "HASH" } //Partition key
    ],
    AttributeDefinitions: [
      { AttributeName: "LastName", AttributeType: "S" }
    ],
    ProvisionedThroughput: {
      ReadCapacityUnits: 10,
      WriteCapacityUnits: 10
    }
  };
  dynamodb.createTable(params, function (err, data) {
    if (err) {
      console.error("Unable to create table. Error JSON:", JSON.stringify(err, null, 2));
    }
    else {
      console.log("Created table. Table description JSON:", JSON.stringify(data, null, 2));
    }
  });
};
```

The AWS SDK will be used in a similar way in some of our demos in the next chapter. It would be a good idea to look over the API documentation to get a better understanding of how these services are created and how they can be used throughout your applications.

Azure SDK

Similar to the AWS SDK, Azure also has an SDK that you can use when creating your Azure functions. The list of available SDKs for different tools and platforms includes these:

- .NET
- Java
- Node.js
- PHP
- Python
- Ruby
- Mobile
- Media
- Android
- iOS
- JavaScript
- Swift
- Windows

Since we will be using a Node.js runtime to create our applications in the following demos, we will continue to look at examples of using SDKs with JavaScript. You can get the Azure SDK by using the command npm install azure. Just as with AWS, Node Package Manager will install the Azure development kit for you. If you only want to install individual modules for specific services, you can do this through NPM as well. The following code shows how to easily create a database in DocumentDB utilizing the Azure SDK:

```
var DocumentClient = require('documentdb').DocumentClient;
var host = 'host';
var key = 'key';
var dbClient = new DocumentClient(host, {masterKey: key});
var databaseDefinition = { id: 'myDatabase' };

//Create Database
client.createDatabase(databaseDefinition, function(err, database) {
    if(err) return console.log(err);
    console.log('Database Created');
});
```

This JavaScript utilizes the DocumentDB client to create and instantiate a new DocumentDB database in Azure. The require statement collects the module from Azure and allows you to perform multiple DocumentDB operations straight from your function. We will be using this in more detail in the Azure tutorials.

Google Cloud SDK

Google Cloud's SDK also supports various tools and platforms:

- Java
- Python
- Node.js
- Ruby
- GO
- .NET
- PHP

However, since Google Cloud Functions supports only Node.js at the moment, the Node.js SDK for Google Cloud is what we will be using to implement serverless applications. The Cloud SDK has many features that deserve further explanation.

The gcloud tool manages authentication, local configuration, developer workflow, and interactions with the Cloud Platform APIs. The gsutil tool provides command-line access to manage Cloud Storage buckets and objects. Kubectl orchestrates the deployment and management of Kubernetes container clusters on gcloud. Bq allows you to run queries, manipulate datasets, tables, and entities in BigQuery through the command line. You can use these tools to access Google Compute Engine, Google Cloud Storage, Google BigQuery, and other services from the command line.

With the gcloud tool, you can start and manage different Cloud SDK emulators built for Google Cloud Pub/Sub and Google Cloud Datastore. This means you will have the ability to simulate these services in your local environment for testing and validation.

You also have the ability to install language-specific client libraries through the Cloud SDK. To install the Cloud SDK for Node.js, enter the following command into your terminal: npm install –save google-cloud. Google Cloud also recommends you install the command-line SDK tools. To do this, you can install the SDK specific for your machine from this site: https://cloud.google.com/sdk/docs/. The following code demonstrates how to use the Google Cloud SDK for Node.js to upload a file to cloud storage.

```
var googleCloud = require('google-cloud')({
 projectId: 'my-project-id',
 keyFilename: '/path/keyfile.json'
});

var googleStorage = googleCloud.storage();
var backups = googleStorage.bucket('backups');
backups.upload('file.zip', function(err, file) {
});
```

The JavaScript requires the google-cloud module, which enables you to utilize and alter different Google Cloud services in your code. While this SDK isn't as integrated as the AWS and Azure SDKs, it is growing and can be used to create and deploy functions as well as other services.

Developing Locally vs. Using the Console

How should you start developing your serverless application? Do you build it locally and then deploy it to the cloud provider, or do you build it within the cloud provider's console? A mixture? This section discusses best practices and options for developing locally and within the provider's environment.

Local Development

Developing locally is often preferable because it means you get to use the tools, IDEs, and environments you are used to. However, the tricky part about developing locally can be knowing how to package and deploy your functions to the cloud so that you spend less time figuring this out and more time working on your code logic. Knowing best practices for project structure and testing can help speed up the development process while still letting you develop using your own tools.

For AWS Lambda functions, it is important to remember that the handler function must be in the root of the zip folder. This is where AWS looks to execute your function when it's triggered. Structuring your project in a way that enforces this execution rule is necessary. For testing locally, the NPM package `lambda-local` allows you to create and store test events that you can execute on your function locally before taking the time to deploy to AWS. If you aren't using a framework that automates this deployment for you, using a package such as `lambda-local` is preferred.

Azure also offers an NPM package that can test your functions locally. Azure Functions Core Tools is a local version of the Azure Functions runtime that allows you to create, run, debug, and publish functions locally.

■ **Note**   The Azure NPM package currently works only on Windows.

Visual Studio offers tools for Azure functions that provide templates, the ability to run and test functions, and a way to publish directly to Azure. These tools are fairly advanced and give you a lot of the function right out of the box. Some limitations of these tools include limited IntelliSense, inability to remove additional files at destination, and inability to add new items outside of the file explorer.

Google Cloud has an Alpha release of a cloud functions local emulator. The emulator currently allows you to run, debug, and deploy your functions locally before deploying them to the cloud directly.

Deployment of Functions and Resources

There are several options for deployment from a local environment to a cloud environment. Using the Serverless Framework is a preferred method because it builds condensed deployment packages that are provider-specific so you can use them to build the same application in any account. It is also preferred because it allows you to create dependent services and security simultaneously.

Another option for deploying from your local environment to the cloud is using the provider's command-line interfaces. AWS, Azure, and Google Cloud all offer CLIs that can be installed and utilized to create and deploy various services. The AWS CLI can be installed if you have Python and `pip` using this command:

```
pip install --upgrade --user awscli.
```

Once the CLI is installed you can configure your AWS CLI account using the command:

```
aws configure
```

The documentation for this can be found at `http://docs.aws.amazon.com/cli/latest/userguide/installing.html`

This configuration will ask you for your AWS Access Key ID, AWS Secret Access Key, Default region name, and default output format. Once these values are configured, you can use the CLI to create and configure your AWS services. For a complete list of services and CLI commands, go to `https://docs.aws.amazon.com/cli/latest/reference.`

Azure also offers a command-line interface as well as PowerShell commands to manage and deploy your Azure resources. To install the Azure CLI with a `bash` command, use:

```
curl -L https://aka.ms/InstallAzureCli | bash
```

Azure has also released a Cloud Shell, an interactive, browser-accessible shell for managing Azure resources. Cloud Shell can be launched from the Azure portal and allows you to have a browser-accessible, shell experience without having to manage or provision the machine yourself. This enables you to create and manage Azure scripts for resources easily. To get started with the Cloud Shell, I recommend following the tutorial provided by Microsoft at `https://docs.microsoft.com/en-us/azure/cloud-shell/quickstart.`

Google Cloud also takes advantage of a CLI within a Cloud Shell that allows you to access and deploy local resources. This allows you to manage projects and resources without having to install the Cloud SDK or other tools locally. To utilize the Google Cloud Shell, all you have to do is enable it from the console. To initiate the Cloud Shell, you simply enable it in the console as you would do for Azure. Figure 2-8 shows an example of enabling the Cloud Shell.

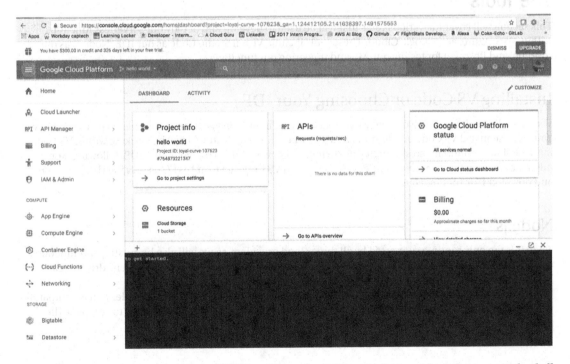

Figure 2-8. *The Google Cloud Shell is enabled by clicking the shell icon in the top right; it then runs in the shell screen at the bottom*

You can use any of these tools to develop and configure your serverless functions and associated resources. For consistency, we will use the Serverless Framework, which is accessible to all three providers we will be exploring.

Developing and Testing in the Cloud Console

Developing functions in the cloud console tends to be a little trickier than developing locally. One good thing about developing in the console is that you don't have to worry about deploying the functions; all you have to do is test and save them. Azure allows you to navigate through your project structure and make changes in the console. AWS allows you to look at your handler file as long as your deployment package isn't too large to enable inline editing. Google Cloud also allows inline editing for smaller deployment packages.

Each of the cloud providers also lets you specify test cases that you can store and use to test your functions as you make changes to them. They also provide monitoring and logging that you don't necessarily get locally. This provides developers with a history of insight into their functions and how they respond to different events.

Establishing triggers can also be easier in the cloud provider environment. AWS, Azure, and Google make it very easy to assign a trigger to a function within the console. They also provide templated test cases that can be used to test functions right out of the box. As these providers' serverless platforms grow in capabilities and functionality, I can imagine developing in the console becoming much more common. For now, the preferred method is to develop locally using your tools and IDEs and rely on advanced deployment tools to deploy and test in the cloud. This could also be dictated by the size of your business. For instance, larger businesses may prefer you to use in-place development environments, whereas when developing on your own you can create within the console without any constraints.

The Tools

This section will cover the various tools that will be used to develop and deploy our serverless functions within AWS, Azure, and Google Cloud. These tools include Visual Studio Code as our IDE, Node.js as our runtime, and Postman for testing our API and triggering our functions.

Installing VS Code or Choosing Your IDE

Visual Studio Code is my IDE of choice for its ease of use, built-in insights, and cross-platform accessibility. You can also install VS Code on Windows or Mac, which is a great feature. I will be working within VS Code for the following tutorials; so although you are more than welcome to use your own IDE, following along might be easier in the same environment. To download VS Code, go to `https://code.visualstudio.com/` and download for your machine.

Node.js

Node.js is the only runtime supported by all three cloud providers, so we will also be creating our functions using Node. Besides being the only runtime that is completely supported, Node is an event-driven, scalable JavaScript that fits the need for building lightweight, scalable functions.

To install Node, navigate to `https://nodejs.org/en/download/` and find the installer that is compatible with your machine. It takes little time to download the installer and then follow its steps to complete the node installation. Figure 2-9 shows the Node.js download options.

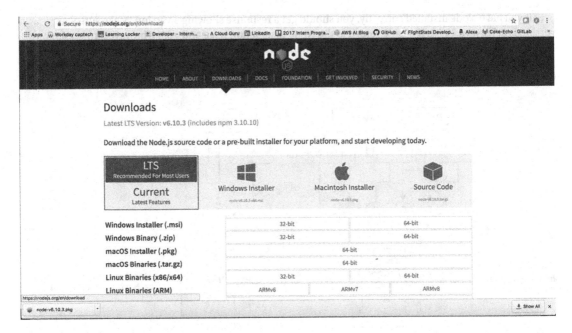

Figure 2-9. *The nodejs download page allows you to download node for Windows or for Mac platforms. It also allows you to choose the install method and package.*

After you have installed Node.js, navigate to your terminal (for Mac) or command prompt (for Windows) and check to confirm that the installation worked, by running the command node –v. Figure 2-10 shows the result.

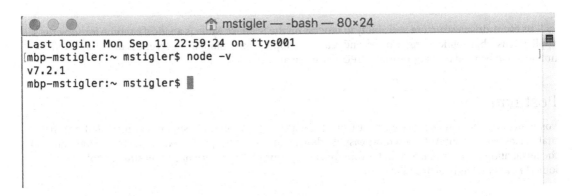

Figure 2-10. *This terminal command confirms that I do have Node installed. The –v flag signifies version, so the response that returns is the version of Node I have installed.*

If you have Node installed correctly, you should get a response showing a version. Make sure your version is at least v0.10.32. If it isn't, return to the Node installation page and grab a more recent version.

Now that we have Node installed, we can begin to use it in our serverless demos. To expand on what Node.js is and how it works, Figure 2-11 demonstrates how it operates under the hood to support thousands of concurrent connections.

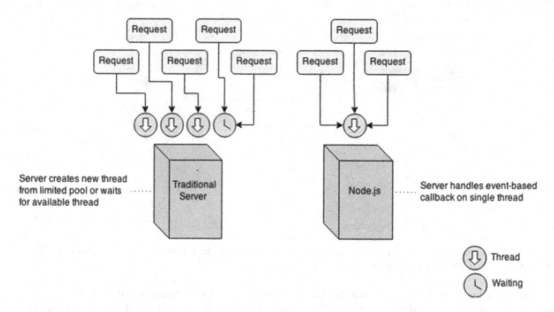

Figure 2-11. *This figure from havlena.net illustrates the concurrency of Node.js established by its single-thread approach*

Its event-driven structure and ability to process on the fly make Node.js an ideal runtime for serverless applications, chat applications, proxies, and real-time applications. Similar to serverless functions, Node is not meant to be used for long-running, CPU-intensive operations.

Postman

Postman is another handy tool we will be using throughout the tutorials. Postman is a cross-platform GUI that makes testing your APIs incredibly easy. To download it, go to https://www.getpostman.com/ and click the installation package that is right for your machine. Figure 2-12 shows what the Postman application looks like after it has been installed.

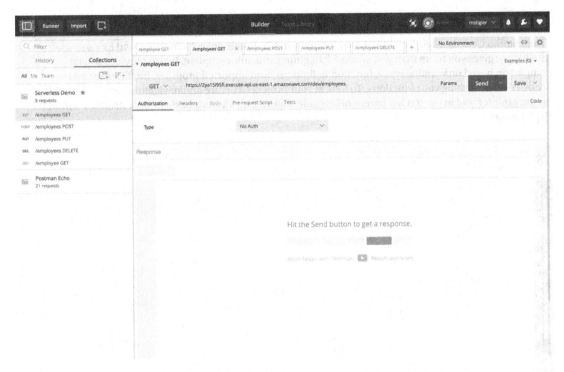

Figure 2-12. This figure shows the Postman application and everything you can do within it

Postman allows you to save requests so you can easily access them the next time you want to test them. To hit an API, you specify the method, the endpoint, and any parameters, and click Send. This will call the API and return any information it gets back to Postman.

We will be using this tool throughout the book to trigger our functions that are being executed by API requests. Postman will feed us the results of the requests in the Response section of the application.

Environment Setup

For the rest of this book, we will be walking through several function examples using AWS, Azure, and Google Cloud. To accomplish this, I recommend a set of tools to be used so that development environments are the same throughout the tutorials. I will be using Visual Studio Code as an IDE, a Node.js runtime using Node Package Manager (NPM), and the Serverless Framework to deploy our functions.

Navigating VS Code

Visual Studio Code is a lightweight IDE that has built-in Git, Intellisense, Debugging, and Extensions. Intellisense gives you more than just syntax highlighting and autocomplete. It also provides smart completion based on variable types, function definitions, and imported modules. Intellisense can be accessed while writing your functions. To look at your project structure and navigate between files, click on the explorer tool in the top left corner of VS Code. Figure 2-13 shows a basic project structure within the Explorer tool.

Figure 2-13. *This figure illustrates the Explorer view, where you can navigate through your project and write functions in the workspace*

The built-in Git makes it easy to initialize a repo and use all Git commands right from Visual Studio Code. Figure 2-14 shows the built-in Git component.

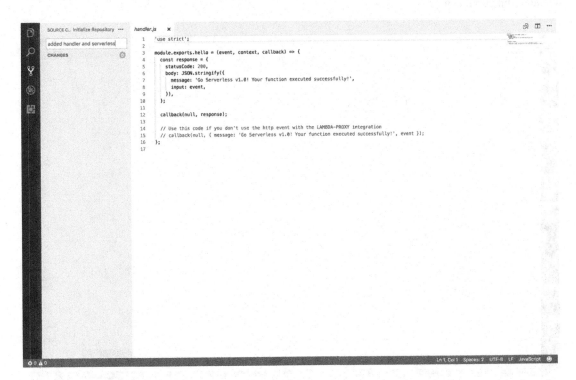

Figure 2-14. *The built-in Git component allows you to initialize a repo, commit and push changes, and track branches. The blue bar across the bottom of VSCode tells you what branch you're in and displays any warnings or errors for that branch*

Visual Studio Code also provides a debugging component that helps you add configurations to your project to step through and debug your code. Figure 2-15 shows the debugging component and a newly created configuration for it.

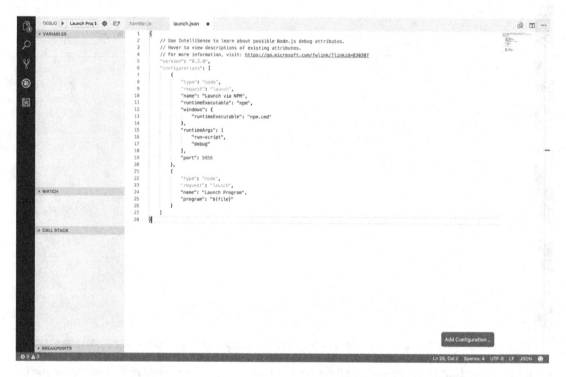

Figure 2-15. *The debugging tool includes breakpoints, configurations, a variable section that you can track, the call stack, and a watch log*

VSCode also provides an extensions section that allows you to install and add different extensions to your project. One extension we will be using is the *npm* extension for support for Node Package Manager. We can go ahead and install this extension now by navigating to the extensions component and searching for NPM in the marketplace. Figure 2-16 shows how to locate the NPM extension.

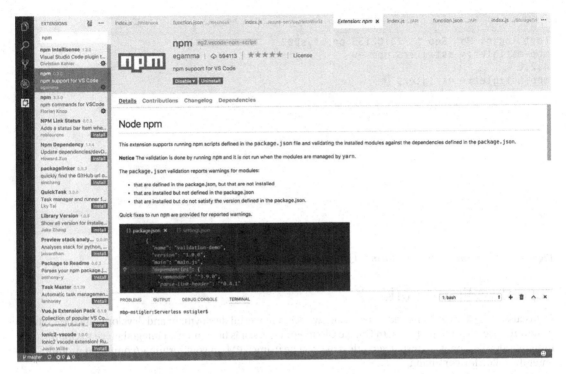

Figure 2-16. *The NPM extension that we would like to install to set up our environment can be found in the marketplace. You can install it by clicking the Install option.*

The extensions will give you the details, change log, and dependencies along with examples of how they will be used. For the purpose of the following tutorials, we will go ahead and install the NPM extension that allows you to run commands in code as well as the extensions that provide support for VS code.

Node Package Manager: What It Does and How to Use It

Node Package Manager is a package manager for JavaScript so we will be using it with our Node.js applications to install various packages that are needed to complete our project. NPM is very collaborative, allowing you to install, share, and distribute code. NPM includes packages such as gulp, grunt, bower, async, lodash, and request.

NPM is installed along with Node, so we can go ahead and use our terminal/command prompt to see if we do indeed have NPM installed. Use the command npm -version to see if you have npm installed. Figure 2-17 shows a response from the terminal that indicates the version of npm I have installed.

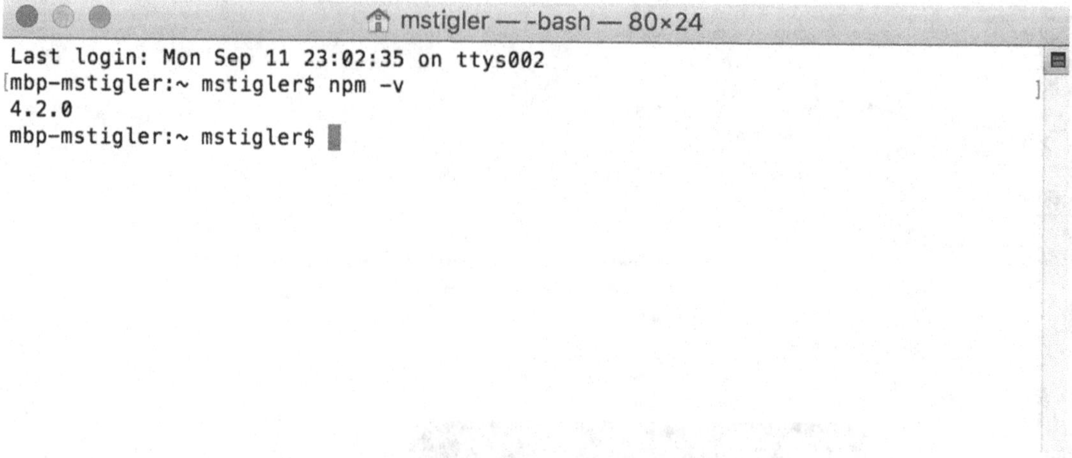

```
● ● ●                    ⌂ mstigler — -bash — 80×24
Last login: Mon Sep 11 23:02:35 on ttys002
[mbp-mstigler:~ mstigler$ npm -v
4.2.0
mbp-mstigler:~ mstigler$ ▮
```

Figure 2-17. The npm version returned 4.2.0, indicating that I do have NPM installed

Serverless Framework

As discussed in Chapter 1, the Serverless Framework is a powerful deployment and development tool. With its new release of its integration with Google Cloud Functions, it is becoming an integral piece to cloud functions development. To install Serverless, we will be using NPM. In your terminal/command prompt, enter the following command:

```
npm install -g serverless
```

This will install Serverless globally on your machine. So when we create different function projects later on, we can quickly and easily create new services and deploy them using Serverless. For more information before then, `https://serverless.com/framework/docs/` provides documentation for Serverless for each of the cloud providers we cover.

Organizing your Development Environment

There are many ways to organize our development environment; however, since we will be developing serverless applications with three different cloud providers, it makes the most sense to organize by provider and then demonstrate how to develop a project that is provider-agnostic.

To start, I recommend setting up a Git repository or some sort of version control. You can get a free account on GitHub to store your code by going to `http://www.github.com`. I created a repository called Serverless and then created three projects within it (AWS, Azure, and Google). For each project, I initialized a serverless framework project within it. Inside your AWS project folder, run the command:

```
serverless create --template aws-nodejs --path aws-service.
```

The template defines which cloud provider you are using along with the runtime. The path defines the name of the service you are creating. I chose to name my service `aws-service`. After creating the service, we need to install the project dependencies within the service. Navigate within the service and run the following command:

```
npm install
```

As we have seen before, Node Package Manager will read the package.json file provided by Serverless and will install all listed dependencies. Figure 2-18 shows the project structure the Serverless Framework gives you out of the box.

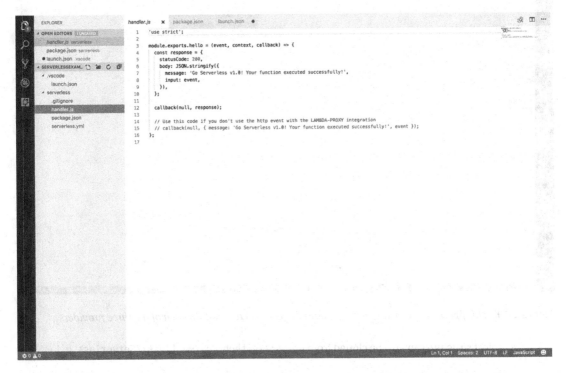

Figure 2-18. *The Serverless Framework creates a package.json file, a sample handler.js file, and a serverless.yml file when it is installed*

Inside the same repository, we are also going to install Serverless in the Azure and Google projects. For Azure, we enter the command:

```
serverless create --template azure-nodejs --path azure-service.
npm install
```

This accomplishes the same thing that we did with AWS. If you open up your Azure project in Visual Studio Code, you should see the same project structure (handler.js, serverless.yml, package.json, and node_modules). We will continue to do the same thing with the Google project.

```
serverless create --template google-nodejs --path google-service.
npm install
```

Figure 2-19 shows a finished project skeleton with each of the three cloud providers. We will be using the serverless.yml file in the next three chapters to deploy our serverless functions within each provider's environment.

Figure 2-19. *This figure demonstrates a bare-bones project structure within each of the three providers*

This project structure can also be cloned from `https://github.com/mgstigler/Serverless.git`.

Conclusion

In this chapter we covered everything you need to know to begin building serverless functions. We have the tools and environment set up, as well as the knowledge of how triggers, events, and functions come together to produce scalable, event-based applications. In the next chapter, we will go through some examples of building functions using AWS Lambda.

CHAPTER 3

■ ■ ■

Amazon Web Services

In this chapter, we will utilize Amazon Web Services (AWS) to create several serverless applications. We will use Lambda to create a Hello World function that is triggered by a test case that we'll create. We will also use API Gateway resources and methods to trigger a Lambda function with RESTful HTTP requests that will return data from DynamoDB. Finally, we will explore a triggered storage application, where we are able to resize images uploaded to Amazon's S3 service using a Lambda function. By the end of this chapter, we will have three serverless applications and experience with several AWS services.

■ **Note**   DynamoDB is Amazon's NoSQL Cloud Database Service. We will use this and S3 (Simple Storage Service, Amazon's blob storage) to get experience with two different storage options and their place in serverless applications.

Explore the UI

Before we begin writing our applications, we will go over the AWS UI and how to navigate it, various pricing options, and the Lambda portal. After signing into the console at `http://www.console.aws.amazon.com`, your home will display a list of AWS Services. Figure 3-1 gives you an idea of all of the services AWS provides.

© Maddie Stigler 2018
M. Stigler, *Beginning Serverless Computing*, https://doi.org/10.1007/978-1-4842-3084-8_3

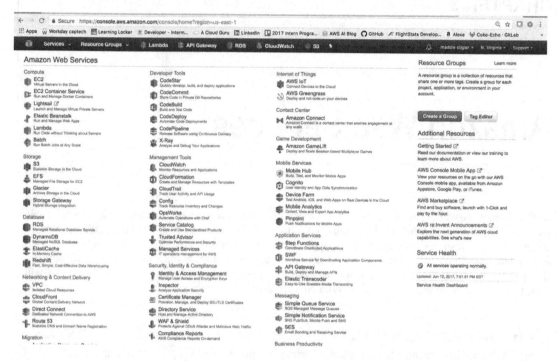

Figure 3-1. *AWS provides several services spanning different topics and abilities, including compute, storage, database, and application services. We can access these under the Services tab across the top. We can also pin favorite services by clicking the pin across the navigation bar and adding the service to it. I have my most used services pinned for easy access.*

Navigation

Outside of accessing AWS Services, we also have access to AWS *resource groups* from the portal. A resource group is a collection of resources that share one or more tags. Resource groups are good for keeping project services separated and organized. A resource group can easily be created from the Resource Groups tab across the top. You can also create resource groups from the panel on the right.

The Services tab will allow you to search and sort services that you see on the home page. AWS also provides Additional Resources to help you get started using AWS, and a Service Health check on the right panel that lets you see the health of your services right on login. The bell in the top banner provides you with alerts given by AWS. These alerts give you any open issues, any future scheduled changes, and any other notifications.

Under your username, you can access your account, your organization, billing dashboard, organization, and sign out. Figure 3-2 shows these options and where to access them. We will look into the billing dashboard more in the Pricing section of this chapter. AWS Organizations enables you to apply policy-based controls centrally across multiple accounts in the AWS Cloud. You can consolidate all your AWS accounts into an organization, and arrange all AWS accounts into distinct organizational units.

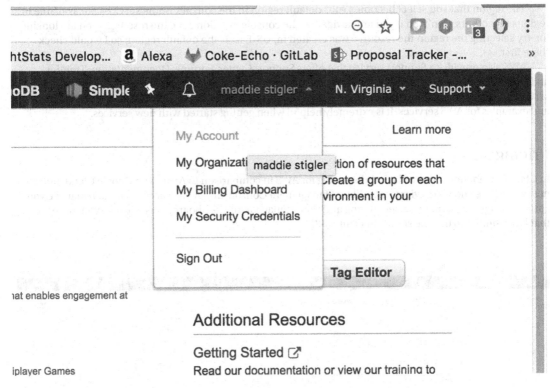

Figure 3-2. Your username and account information can all be accessed straight from the home page on the portal. This is where you can manage all of your account settings and billling information.

The region to the right of your username allows you to select the Amazon Region you are working in. The Region Names are as follows:

- US East (Ohio)
- US East (N. Virginia)
- US West (N. California)
- US West (Oregon)
- Canada (Central)
- Asia Pacific (Mumbai)
- Asia Pacific (Seoul)
- Asia Pacific (Singapore)
- Asia Pacific (Tokyo)
- EU (Frankfort)
- EU (Ireland)
- EU (London)
- South America (Sao Paulo)

The region that you select becomes your default region in the console. Some services are available in regions that others aren't. So if you are navigating the console and don't see the resources you are looking for, try selecting the region the resource was created in. US-East is the default region, so I would check there first.

AWS also provides a Support service that offers Support Center, Forums, Documentation, Training, and Other Resources. These are good for learning new services and getting hands-on experience with new services. The documentation provides a Getting Started guide with examples, SDKs and Tools, resources, and examples for AWS services. It is extremely helpful when getting started with new services.

Pricing

In Chapter 1, Table 1-1 showed Lambda pricing for AWS in comparison to Azure and Google Cloud, but now you will see how to navigate the Billing Management Console under your account to help manage your costs. Under your username, select Billing and Cost Management Dashboard. This will take you to a page that looks similar to the one shown in Figure 3-3.

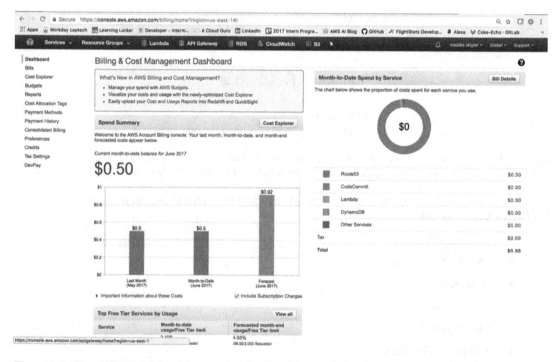

Figure 3-3. *Your Billing and Cost Management dashboard gives you an overview of your costs per month, per service, and as a forecast*

AWS gives you a lot of accessibility with managing costs of services, payment methods, generating reports, and viewing your bills. All of these capabilities are available through the Billing dashboard on the left panel. The Billing option lets you sort through your AWS bills by month. It provides a history of these bills as well as a CSV export option. Figure 3-4 demonstrates this capability.

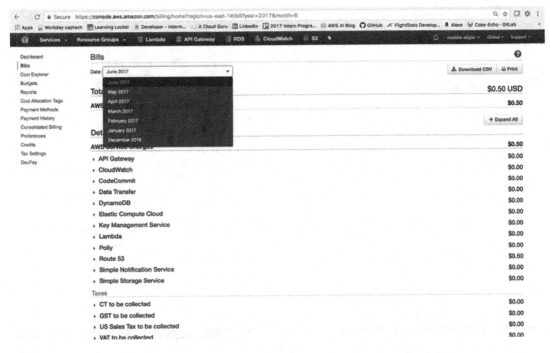

Figure 3-4. The Bills section allows you to sort through your bills and view them based on date

Another important billing capability is Consolidated Billing, which allows you to handle multiple accounts under one master account. It works with AWS Organizations to create multiple organizations, organize accounts in these organizations, and apply policies to these organizations. A good use case for this is a large company with multiple projects. Instead of using resource groups and tags, you can keep your AWS applications and resources completely separated from one another with Organizations and Consolidated Billing.

Another solution is to set up billing alerts within the billing console. Billing alerts will send you email notifications when your account hits a certain dollar amount or resource amount set by you. I made the mistake of thinking all services in the free tier were free and was hit with a pretty hefty bill after spinning up multiple RDS instances and EC2 instances. Since then, I have set my billing alerts to notify me when I go over $1.

Lambda

The Lambda console can be accessed from the Services tab across the top, under Computing. The Lambda dashboard lets you view the number of functions, the total code storage, account-level metrics over the past 24 hours, and what's new within Lambda. Figure 3-5 gives you an overview of a Lambda dashboard.

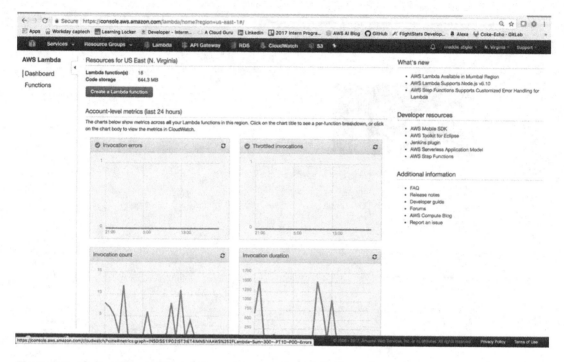

Figure 3-5. *The Lambda dashboard gives you an overview of all of your functions*

The Functions section is where you go to access and create Lambda functions. Figure 3-6 shows the Functions UI.

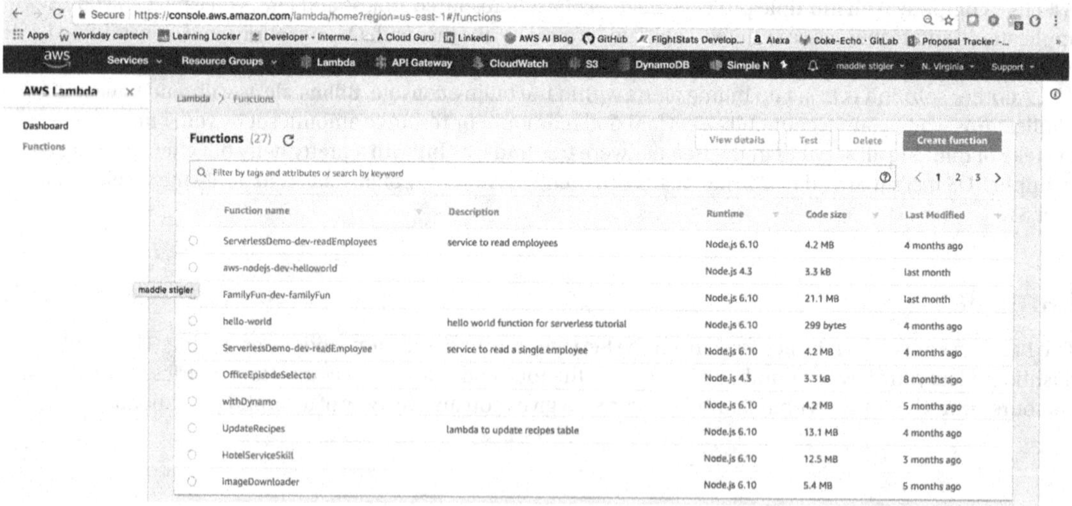

Figure 3-6. *The Lambda Functions screen shows all of your functions at a high level. You can click on a function to access the code, test events, and configurations.*

We will explore the Lambda portal and all of its capabilities in more detail as we begin creating our Lambda functions. However, before we can create our functions we will need to configure our IAM (Identity and Access Management). It is important to note that setting up IAM services is not required for using functions, but we are following best practices and it is in your best interest to go ahead and follow the next couple of steps. We will dive into more advanced examples later that will require the use of IAM to use different services.

Security IAM

The IAM service is an incredibly important and integrated service within AWS. IAM lets you assign users, roles, and policies in order to help secure your Amazon resources.

IAM Console

The IAM console is found under Services and Security, Identity, and Compliance. The console gives you a dashboard, groups, users, roles, policies, identity providers, account settings, a credential report, and encryption keys. From the dashboard (Figure 3-7), you can access a user's sign-in link. This is where users who are not admin users are directed to log in. It also gives you an overview of your IAM Resources, including the number of users, groups, customer-managed policies, roles, and identity providers.

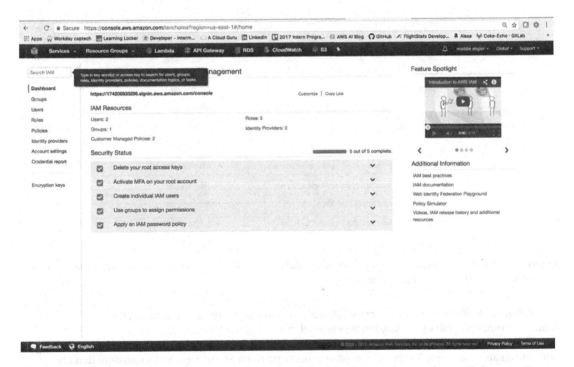

Figure 3-7. *The IAM dashboard gives you an overview of all of your IAM resources along with five security steps you are recommended to complete*

To begin, it is important to complete the five steps listed in the Security Status console: deleting your root access keys, activating MFA (multi-factor authentication) on your root account, creating individual IAM users, creating groups for permissions, and applying an IAM password policy. By following these steps, you are ensuring that your IAM settings are properly secured so you can begin creating users and roles.

Roles, Policies, and Users

Roles, Policies, and Users are your means to set permissions to people, services, and resources. Roles are created under the Roles tab and allow you to create roles with set policies. These roles can be assigned to users and services. For instance, if I have a group of developers who I want to be able to edit and access Lambda and services, but not root account information, I can create a role called Developers.

After the role is created, I can assign certain policies to it. Policies determine the amount of access a role has to a service. Figure 3-8 demonstrates the Policy console with all of the preconfigured policies. You also have the option to create your own.

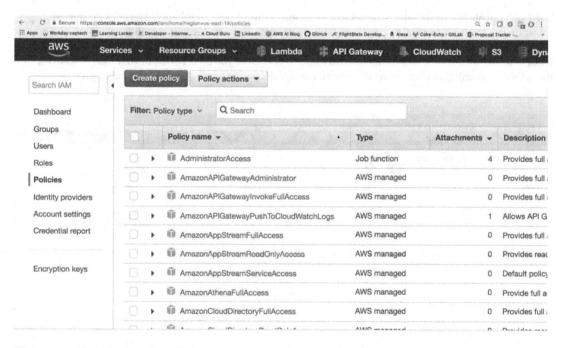

Figure 3-8. *The Policies section allows you to create and assign policies. The attachments describe the entities (users and services).associated with a policy.*

Policies describe the amount of access allowed to a particular service. For instance, the AdminstratorAccess policy gives you full access to all resources for all services.

The Users window lets you add users to AWS. They are given their own login and whatever roles and policies you attach to them. To access the console, users are given Access Keys and a password that are downloaded by CSV or sent directly to them. You determine the amount of time they have with the default password and all of the password policies regarding their user login.

You also have the ability to add users to groups. Groups can be used to make permissions easier. If you have a group of users you want to all have admin access, you can add them to a group so all of the group policies are applied across the board. For the purpose of our serverless applications, we won't be assigning users or groups, but it is good to keep these opportunities in mind as you build bigger applications with a larger group of people.

Roles for Lambda

AWS requires you to assign a role to your Lambda functions. These roles can differ across Lambda functions as they require access to different AWS services. However, just to get started with our Hello World function, we are going to create an AWS Lambda role that can be assigned to our functions.

In the Roles tab, we will click the Create New Role option. We will name our role "lambda_basic_ execution." Under permissions, we will attach the AWSLambdaExecute policy. If you look into this policy, you can see the exact permissions attached to it. The policy allows full access to CloudWatch to log our function, and provides read/write access to AWS S3. Figure 3-9 shows what the role should look like after creating it.

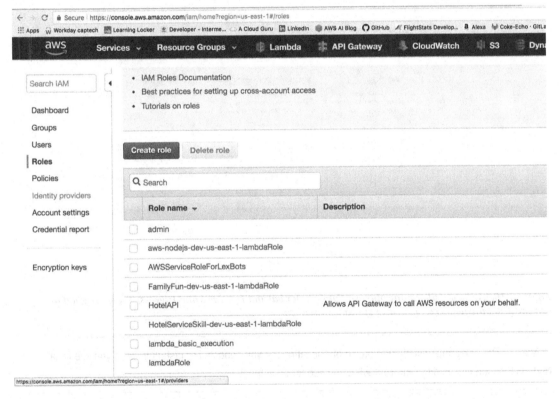

Figure 3-9. The role has the AWSLambdaExecute policy attached to it. You can look into the policy to see the permissions attached, and you can also attach more policies as necessary.

The Role ARN at the top of the console is the Amazon Resource Name. This is what uniquely identifies the role we just created. When we create our first function, we will assign our Lambda to this role, giving it all the permissions specified within the one attached policy.

Your First Code

Now that we have our IAM role set and a good feel for navigating the AWS console, we can begin writing our first code. This Hello World Lambda function is going to give us experience creating a Lambda function, assigning a role to it, creating a test event, executing it, and later viewing the logs in CloudWatch.

Hello World

We will start by creating a new function in the Lambda console. After clicking Create a Lambda Function, you will see a list of blueprint options (Figure 3-10). These blueprints give you a Lambda skeleton that you can edit to complete the functionality you are looking for. To start off, we are just going to select a blank function.

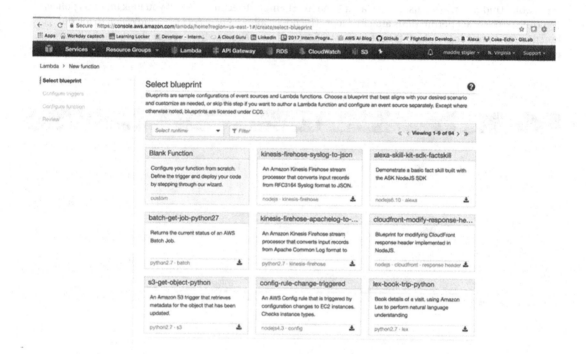

Figure 3-10. *AWS provides many blueprint options for various runtimes and triggers. These are good to explore if you are new to a particular runtime or service.*

■ **Note** The blueprints will change based on the language you choose. For instance, what you see for a Node.js function will be different from what you see for a C# function.

After selecting a blank function, we next have to configure our function. This requires assigning it a name, description, runtime, and a handler and role. Names do not have to be unique universally, just within your functions. I named this `hello-world` and gave it a description and a runtime of Node.js 6.10. AWS also allows you to either edit your code inline or upload a zip. Since this function is going to be simple and small, we can edit it inline. Figure 3-11 shows what your configuration should look like.

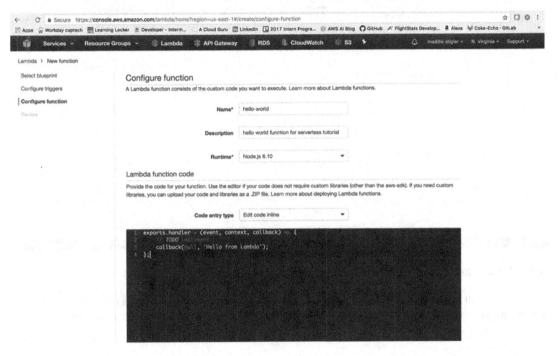

Figure 3-11. *For the purpose of this function, we are just going to have it respond "Hello from Lambda"*

The `exports.handler` defines this as the function handler. It takes in an event (trigger), context, and callback, which is what we will use to signify that the function is finished executing. Our callback is currently responding "Hello from Lambda." Next we need to configure our handler and role. We will leave Environment Variables, Tags, and Advanced Settings blank for now, but feel free to look them over. Our handler is `index.handler`, and our role is the `lambda_basic_execution` role that we created previously. Once this is configured (Figure 3-12), we can move on and create our function.

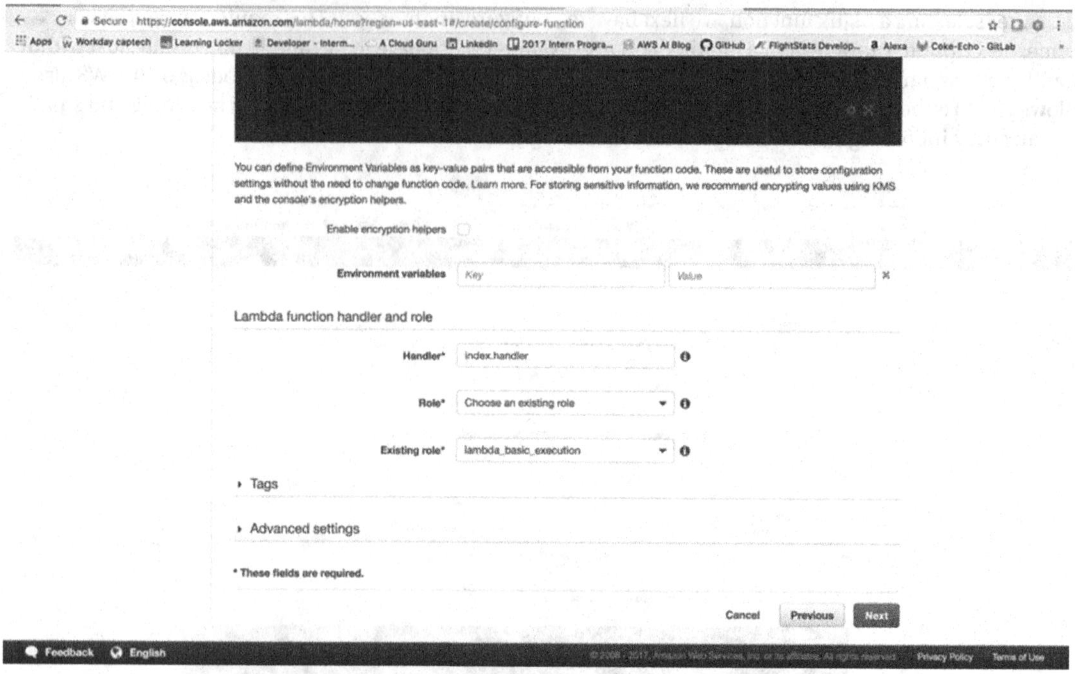

Figure 3-12. *Before moving on, make sure your Lambda function handler and role look like this*

Next, we will look at testing and executing our function. For now, we won't set up a trigger, because that requires trigger configuration. We just want to see what an executing Lambda looks like, how we can create one, and how we can access the logs.

Testing

To test our Lambda function in the console, we can use the Configure Test Event action. Inside the function, if you click Actions, you will see a list of actions you can take on your Lambda:

- Configure Test Event
- Publish New Version
- Create Alias
- Delete Function
- Export Function

We will configure a test event. In the input test event, AWS provides several event templates. Feel free to explore these to see what different incoming events look like. We will use the Hello World event, as shown in Figure 3-13. This event just offers a JSON of various keys and variables.

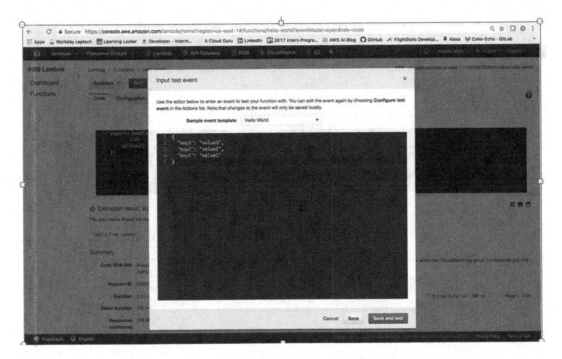

Figure 3-13. *The sample test event template provided by AWS. We will save and test this event.*

Since our Lambda is not configured to do anything specific with the event, we should be able to get our Hello World response from our test event just by triggering it. The test event works the same way a trigger would, causing the Lambda function to execute and respond to the incoming event. You are given options to Save and to Save and Test. With the Save button, the function is not run. Save and Test saves your function and tests it using the provided test case. This is event-driven architecture in action. Figure 3-14 shows the Execution result, Summary, and Log Output.

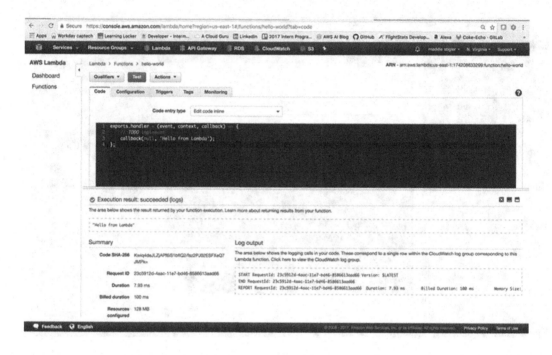

Figure 3-14. *A successful execution with logging*

The execution result demonstrates what we specified our Lambda to do. Since we only specified a callback with a string, that is what we are receiving. The summary shows you the duration of the execution, billed duration, and amount of resources configured. This is important for further configuration of your function. If your Lambda is using only so much memory, that would be a good thing to adjust in its configuration to limit unnecessary space and charges.

We also see the output of the log. Even without explicit logging, we were given the Start of the execution with the request ID and version being run, the End of the request, and a final report. The following demonstrates the code we are running for our Hello World function:

```
exports.handler = (event, context, callback)=>{
  callback(null, JSON.stringify(event));
};
```

Now that we have shown the function executing, let's change it to repeat back the event coming in. Figure 3-15 shows our updated Lambda function.

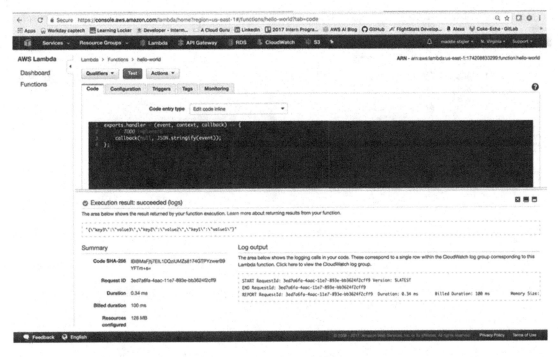

Figure 3-15. *Here the function uses the event coming in to output*

To improve on this Hello World function, try parsing the event and responding to parts of it. Also include inline logging that you can look at in the log output and in CloudWatch.

■ **Tip** Whether or not you're using the console, it is extremely helpful to insert many console.log statements. These let you see what is actually happening within your code and with the data coming in and out, and their output is sent straight to CloudWatch.

CloudWatch

Now, we will examine CloudWatch and see where our logging happens and all of the metrics we get out-of-the-box on our function. In the log output section, navigate to the Click Here option. This will take us to the CloudWatch portal, where our function's logs live. Figure 3-16 shows the two executions I made earlier in this exercise.

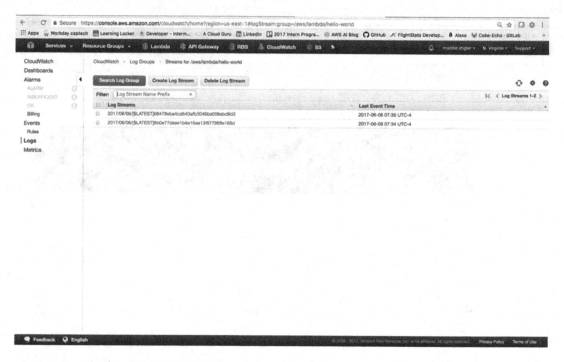

Figure 3-16. *The CloudWatch Log Group for your Lambda keeps your streams for your executions. You can also click on specific streams and investigate logs within that time frame.*

These logs are helpful for analyzing and monitoring your function's executions. In addition to CloudWatch, there is a Monitoring tab in the Lambda function's console that gives you a high-level overview of your function's executions and outputs. To look deeper into a log, click on its stream. This will give you a full detailed log for that execution. Figure 3-17 shows the executions on my Hello World function.

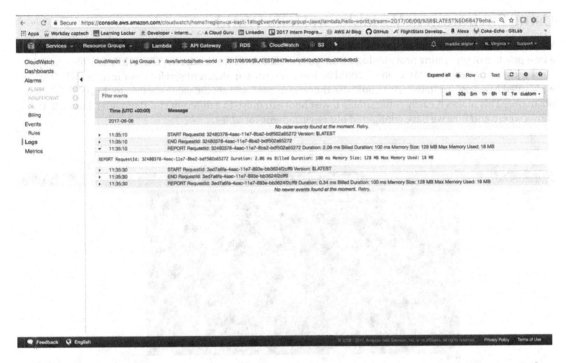

Figure 3-17. *The opened stream gives you detailed UTC time and messages. You can view logs in a particular stream as far back as a week.*

Now that we have become acclimated to the Lambda console, test events, and CloudWatch, we will build upon our Hello World function with environment variables.

The code for the Hello World function can be found at https://github.com/mgstigler/hello-world.git.

Environment Variables

To add onto our Hello World function, we are going to cover environment variables: what they are, how they're used, and how they're configured in AWS.

What Are Environment Variables

Environment variables are those set globally across your serverless application. They are given a key and a value. The value is that of the actual variable, while the key is the name used for that variable throughout the application. The benefit of environment variables is both security and ease of use.

Rather than leaving API keys and various access information scattered throughout your code, you can assign the actual secure variable to an environment variable to be used anonymously. In addition, if you know you are going to be using a variable repeatedly, setting it as an environment variable allows you to access it across your project without re-declaring it. It also allows you to make quick changes in one spot.

To see how environment variables are used, we are going to implement them in our Hello World application.

Using Environment Variables in Hello World

We are going to create an environment variable with the key `provider` and value `AWS`. This also demonstrates a best practice of separating provider logic from your code to prevent vendor lock-in. While for this example we are just using the value AWS, later it could be used to represent different services. For instance, if we knew we wanted to access a database, we could use the key `DB_Host` and set the value specific to the AWS database hostname. This makes it easily configurable if we choose to move to a different cloud provider. Figure 3-18 shows where and how we have configured our environment variables.

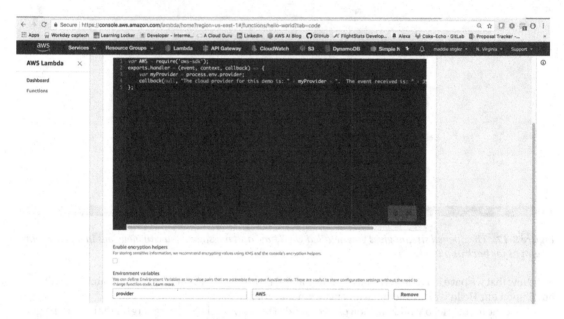

Figure 3-18. *You can configure your environment variables within the AWS Lambda console*

Now we can access this environment variable within our code. Figure 3-19 demonstrates how we reference environment variables and the log output for the execution of the Lambda function.

```
var AWS = require('aws-sdk');
exports.handler = (event, context, callback) => {
  var myProvider = process.env.provider;
  callback(null, "The cloud provider for this demo is: " + myProvider + ". The event
received is: " + JSON.stringify(event));
};
```

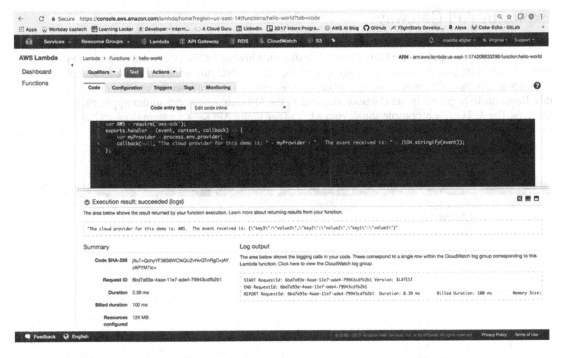

Figure 3-19. *The environment variables are accessed through* `process.env.variable-key`

This shows how easy it is to create and access variables in your code. Now that we have completed a Hello World demonstration of Lambda, we will look at creating a new application that uses an HTTP event and responds to it by returning data from DynamoDB.

HTTP Event

For our first fleshed-out serverless application with Lambda, we are going to use AWS API Gateway to trigger a Lambda function that returns data from a DynamoDB NoSQL Database. API Gateway allows you to create HTTP resources and methods and set them to specific endpoints.

This application will mimic a virtual recipe book. We will create an API Gateway with one resource, Recipes, and one method for that resource, GET. For the endpoint to this GET request, we will set a Lambda function we create, called `GetRecipes`. This function will access a DynamoDB table that we will have prepopulated with recipes and return a JSON value of these recipes as the response. Before setting up our API Gateway, we will go ahead and create our Lambda function, leaving the trigger and code blank for now. Once you have done this, you can move on to exploring API Gateway.

Exploring API Gateway

API Gateway is an AWS service that lets you easily create and access an API all through the API Gateway console. It gives you a public RESTful API interface to a wide host of AWS services. This allows you to interact easily with your databases, messaging services, and Lambda functions through a secure gateway. In addition, it is incredibly easy to set up and create endpoints for. This allows the continuation of rapid development. To begin using API Gateway, navigate to the API Gateway service under Application Services. The API Gateway console shows your APIs, usage plans, API Keys, Custom Domain Names, Client Certificates, and Settings. Figure 3-20 shows an example of the API Gateway Console.

Figure 3-20. *With the API Gateway you can easily access and create APIs and set keys and usage plans for them*

To create an API, simply click Create API. This will take you through the process of setting up your own API. We will create a New API and name it Recipe API. After creating your API, you should be directed to a console that allows you to configure your API (Figure 3-21). We want to add a resource to our API called "recipes."

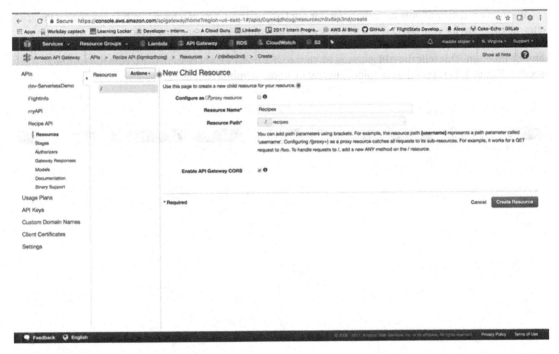

Figure 3-21. *The new child resource can be added to your API resource and will be used in the request URL*

Resources allow you to have multiple objects for your methods. We also want a single GET method attached to our resource. Figure 3-22 shows what your API console should look like after configuring your endpoint.

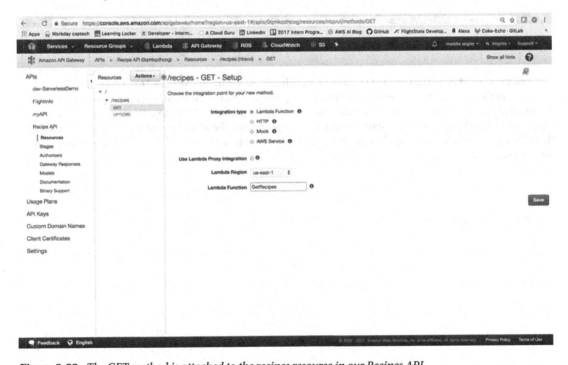

Figure 3-22. *The GET method is attached to the recipes resource in our Recipes API*

We then need to configure an integration for our GET method. You can have Lambda create an API Gateway endpoint for you, but doing it this way gives you control over what the endpoint looks like and its configuration. For this, we want to select the Lambda function, specify the region, and select our GetRecipes Lambda function. This tells the API gateway when the GET method is accessed, to execute the Lambda function. Figure 3-23 shows the complete integration of the Lambda function.

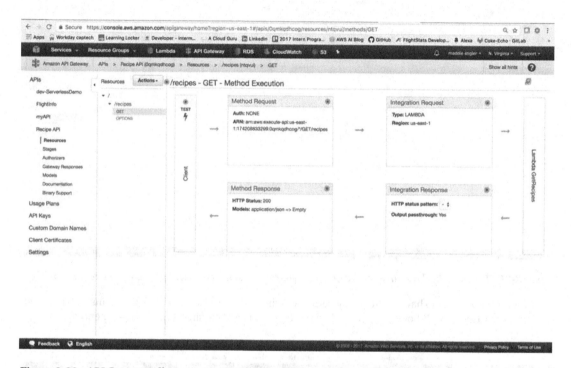

Figure 3-23. *API Gateway allows you to view each method execution within your API*

Before going back to the Lambda console to set this API as our trigger, we need to deploy our API to a stage. Staging is important for version control and deployment. Since we are still in development, we are going to name our stage "Beta." Under Actions, next to Resources, click Deploy. The pop-up shown in Figure 3-24 will ask you to create a stage if you haven't already. Go ahead and create a new stage and name it "beta." Stages represent a unique identifier for a version of a deployed REST API that is callable by different users and services.

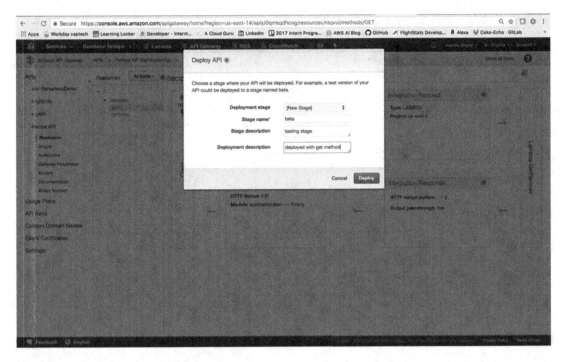

Figure 3-24. *We specify our Stage name when we deploy an API. If we wanted to make changes and see them, we would want to redeploy our API to this stage.*

After deploying, you will be directed to the Stages tab (Figure 3-25). This is where you configure settings for your stage, stage variables, SDK Generation, Swagger exports, Postman extensions, deployment history, and documentation history. Take a look at each of these tabs to see everything that is available to you through API Gateway.

■ **Note**   Swagger is an API framework that allows you to easily view and interact with your endpoints. I like it because it makes it easy to test your services and is also simple to add to your project.

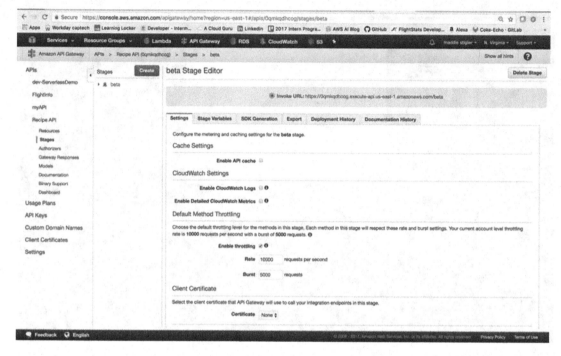

Figure 3-25. *We will use the Invoke URL to test the functionality of our API Gateway as a trigger for Lambda*

At this point, we have an API Gateway with one resource and one method, deployed to a Beta stage, and integrated with our Lambda function. We are ready to set this API as our trigger for our Lambda function and begin responding to requests.

■ **Note** You might be wondering why we are only giving our API one method. Earlier in this book, we discussed the importance of each function having a single task and triggering event. We can add multiple methods to this API, but we would also want to create multiple Lambda functions to respond to the different requests (for example, a Lambda to handle POST requests, a Lambda to handle DELETE requests…).

Using API Gateway as a Trigger

Back in the Lambda function, GetRecipes, we can now configure the API we just created as our trigger. Under Triggers in our function, click Add Trigger. Here, we select API Gateway from the drop-down menu and specify the API we just created. This will tell our Lambda function to wake up to events coming in from this specific service. Figure 3-26 demonstrates the correct configuration for our function.

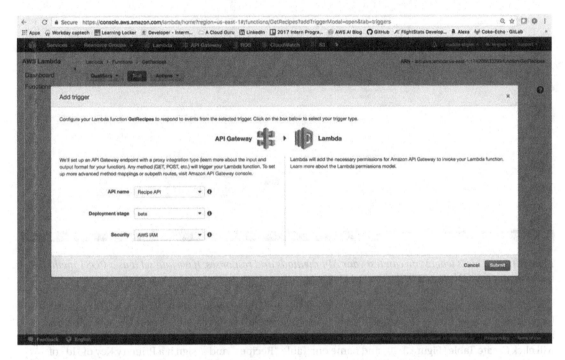

Figure 3-26. *Our Recipe API is configured to trigger our GetRecipes Lambda function*

Leaving the Lambda code as is, we can go into API Gateway and test our trigger. By clicking on the GET resource, we can select Test and test our API (Figure 3-27). Since it is a GET method, it requires no request body. On the right in API Gateway, you should see a response, status, and latency. You could also view this in the browser by just hitting the GET endpoint. The URI for this example is

```
https://lambda.us-east-1.amazonaws.com/2015-03-31/functions/arn:aws:lambda:us-east-
1:174208833299:function:GetRecipes/incovations
```

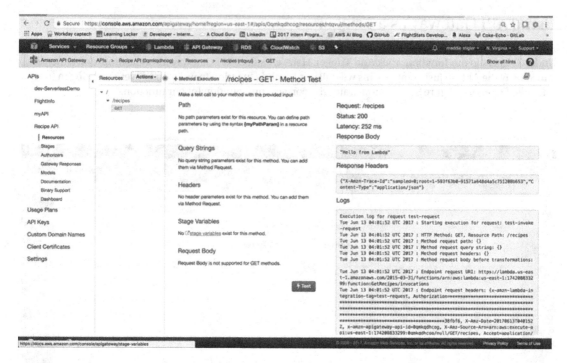

Figure 3-27. *This is where you can test your API methods and responses. If we had set it as a POST method, we could put a JSON request in the request body.*

Now that our trigger is configured, we can develop our Lambda function to respond to this request by returning recipes from a DynamoDB table. To do this, we will first create a DynamoDB table, Recipes, and prepopulate it with some recipes. Use the Services tab to navigate to the DynamoDB service. Here we will click Create Table (Figure 3-28) and name our Table "Recipes" and assign it a Primary Key of "Id" of type "Number." The primary keys should be unique to items. The DynamoDB table consists of items and attributes. In our table, each item is a recipe which has attributes of meal, description, and prep-time.

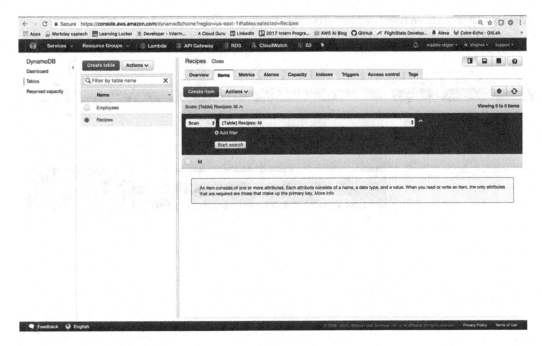

Figure 3-28. *An empty DynamoDB table with a Primary Key of Id*

From here, we will create a couple of recipe items to populate our table. To do this, click Create Item and append fields Meal, Description, and PrepTime with various values (Figure 3-29).

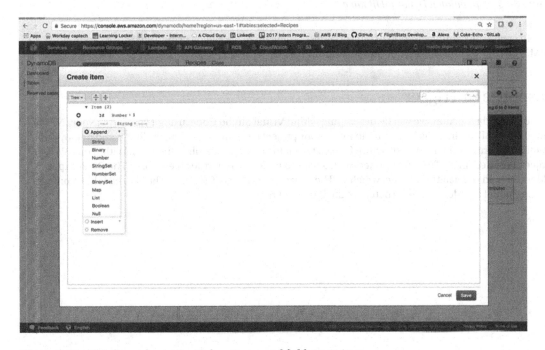

Figure 3-29. *This figure demonstrates how to append fields to an item*

When our table has been populated with a couple of recipes, we can build our Lambda function to return these recipes in the response to the API (Figure 3-30).

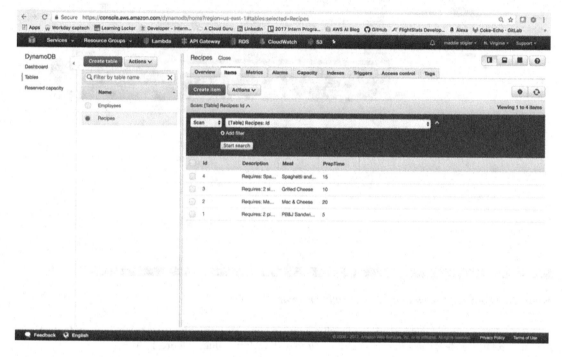

Figure 3-30. *A populated DynamoDB table*

To create the Lambda portion of our serverless application, we will be using TypeScript, Node, and NPM. The next section will go over how to accomplish this.

Response to Trigger

For our Lambda function, we will be developing within Visual Studio Code, using TypeScript, Node, NPM, and the AWS SDK. First, it is important to format our project structure so we can easily zip and deploy our function. Figure 3-31 shows the structure I have chosen to create this Lambda function. Within our AWS project, I created an HTTPTrigger project with a Shared folder and a GetRecipes folder. The GetRecipes folder will hold our handler.js file, which will be triggered by the GET request. The Shared folder contains a Recipes model that defines the structure of the incoming request.

Figure 3-31. *The proposed project structure for the HTTP event*

For now, we will create the function without using the Serverless Framework, so outside of the HTTPTrigger project, we will need a package.json file to specify what NPM installs, and the tsconfig.json file to configure our TypeScript builds. Your package.json file should include aws-sdk and typescript as dependencies.

Listing 3-1. A complete package.json file for this application

```
{
 "name": "aws-nodejs",
 "version": "1.0.0",
 "description": "AWS Lambda sample for the Serverless framework",
 "main": "handler.js",
 "keywords": [
 "aws",
 "serverless"
 ],
 "dependencies": {
 "aws-sdk": "^2.34.0"
 },
 "devDependencies": {
 "@types/aws-lambda": "0.0.9",
 "@types/aws-sdk": "0.0.42",
 "@types/node": "^7.0.12",
 "aws-sdk-typescript": "0.0.3",
 "typescript": "2.1.6",
 "typings": "^1.3.3"
 }
}
```

The tsconfig.json should be configured to build on save and to compile on save. This will compile the JavaScript files for TypeScript files as you save. Listing 3-2 shows the tsconfig.json file.

Listing 3-2. The TypeScript file excludes the node_modules, vscode, git, and serverless files in its build.

```
{
"compilerOptions": {
"module": "commonjs",
"target": "es2015",
"noImplicitAny": false,
"sourceMap": true,
"emitDecoratorMetadata": true,
"experimentalDecorators": true,
"declaration": false,
"listFiles": false,
"moduleResolution": "node",
 "rootDirs": [
 "./"
]
},
"exclude": [
".vscode",
".serverless",
".git",
"node_modules"
],
"compileOnSave": true,
"buildOnSave": true,
"atom": {
"rewriteTsconfig": false
}

}
```

We can now do an NPM install on our project to install all of the node modules we will need to create our Lambda function. This will create a node_modules folder in your project with all of its dependencies. We will also create a recipeModel.ts file (Listing 3-3) in the Shared folder. This model will define the structure of the recipes we created in our DynamoDB table. We can then use this in our handler.js file to format our response to the GET request. In the future, with other requests, you can use this model to format the request.

Listing 3-3. The recipeModel.ts file is used to format requests and responses so they match the structure of our DynamoDB table.

```
export interface RecipeModel {
Id:number,
Description:string,
Meal:string,
PrepTime:number
}
```

In our `handler.ts` file, we will create our `GetRecipes` module that will take in an event, context, and callback (as we have done in our Hello World example) and will utilize `aws-sdk` to communicate with our DynamoDB Table and respond back to our request with a list of recipes. Listing 3-4 demonstrates this handler function, followed by the steps that will let us go into further detail.

Listing 3-4. The `handler.ts` function takes in the HTTP event and responds to it by reaching into DynamoDB and grabbing the full list of recipes.

```
'use strict';
exports.__esModule = true;
var AWS = require("aws-sdk");
module.exports.GetRecipes = function (event, context, callback) {
 console.info("Received event: ", JSON.stringify(event, null, 2));
 var docClient = new AWS.DynamoDB.DocumentClient();
 var table = process.env.TABLE_NAME;
 var response = {
  statusCode: 200,
  message: []
 };
 var params = {
  TableName: table,
  ProjectionExpression: "#id, #m, #d, #pt",
  ExpressionAttributeNames: {
   "#id": "Id",
   "#m": "Meal",
   "#d": "Description",
   "#pt": "PrepTime"
  }
 };
 console.log("Scanning Recipes.");
 docClient.scan(params, onScan);
 function onScan(err, data) {
  if (err) {
   response.statusCode = 500;
   console.error("Unable to scan the table. Error JSON:", JSON.stringify(err, null, 2));
   callback(null, response);
  }
  else if (data == null) {
   response.statusCode = 404;
   callback(null, response);
  }
  else {
   console.log("Scan succeeded.");
   data.Items.forEach(function (recipe) {
    response.message.push(recipe);
   });
   callback(null, response);
  }
 }
};
```

1. Import the AWS SDK and `RecipeModel`.

2. Create a DynamoDB client to communicate with the table.

3. Utilize environment variable for the table name (We will set this variable in AWS).

4. Set the response of the message.

5. Create the table connection with parameters (table name, expressions, attributes).

6. Format response to scan.

We can now compile our TypeScript files into JavaScript files. Once we have created the handler, model, node modules, and compiled our TypeScript, we can compress and upload our application. It is important to remember that the `handler.js` file must remain at the root of your compressed files. The compression must occur at the level shown in Figure 3-32.

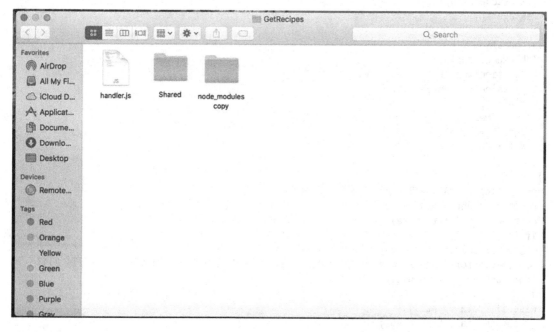

Figure 3-32. *The* `handler.js` *function remains at the root level. We have included only the Shared and* `node_modules` *folders, because that is all that is necessary in this compression.*

After uploading the zip file to our `GetRecipes` Lambda, there are still a couple of configurations to take care of. First, we need to update our handler. Our handler should now be listed as `handler.GetRecipes`. This is because the module we are exporting is called `GetRecipes` and it is found in the `handler.js` file. We should also add our environment variable `TABLE_NAME` with its proper value. We also need to add a policy that gives us access to DynamoDB to our Lambda role. This can be done in AWS IAM under Roles. Finally, we can test our Lambda function using Postman and the URL given to us in the API Staging console. Figure 3-33 demonstrates a Postman request and the response we get back.

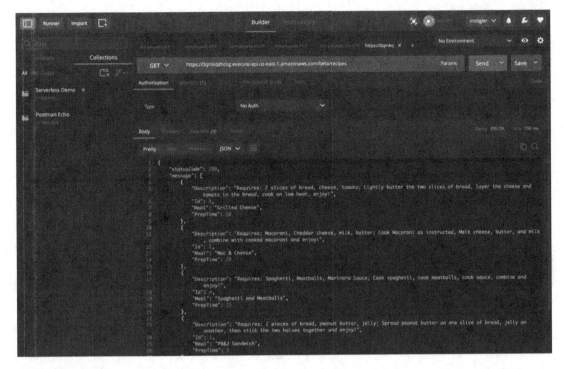

Figure 3-33. *We use the URL provided in API Gateway to make a GET request. Our response is a JSON response with all of our recipes listed.*

We now have a start-to-finish serverless application using API Gateway, Lambda, and DynamoDB.

IMPROVING OUR SERVERLESS FUNCTION

Improve by separating logic and utilizing Serverless Framework

Separate AWS logic from handler:

1. Use Environment variables for AWS specific logic or move AWS logic to shared folder

2. Create Services folder that is specific to AWS and serves DynamoDB data

Utilize the Serverless Framework:

1. Follow instructions for AWS setup on Serverless Framework.

2. Develop and deploy function using Serverless instead of manually.

The code for both of these improvements to the project can be found here: `https://github.com/mgstigler/Serverless/tree/master/AWS/aws-service/HTTPTrigger`

In the next section, we will use the skills and tools we learned with the HTTP Trigger to create a separate Lambda function triggered by a storage event.

Storage Event

In this section we will use a storage event to trigger a Lambda function that responds to the PUT request. The purpose of this application will build from our previous recipe example. Now, we would like to provide pictures of our recipes along with a description, meal, and prep time. To do this, we will use S3 (Simple Storage Service) as our trigger, and a Lambda function that appends a recently uploaded image's URL to the recipe it is associated with.

Amazon S3

AWS offers many storage options ranging from Relational Databases, to NoSQL Databases, to Blob storage. In this exercise, we are going to explore using AWS S3, blob storage, as a trigger for a Lambda function. Within the S3 service, let's create a bucket. Your current S3 console will look something like Figure 3-34.

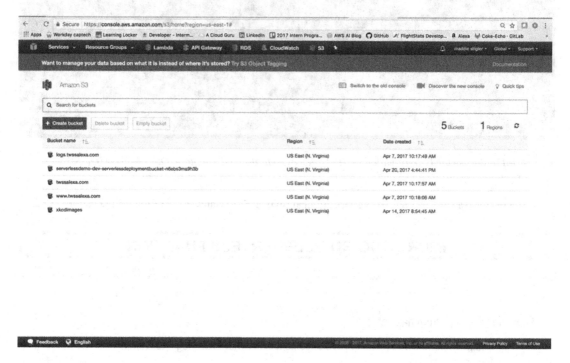

Figure 3-34. *The S3 console lets you view all of your currently active buckets, create new buckets, and search for buckets*

As shown in Figure 3-35, I'm naming mine `recipe-images-ms`. Bucket names are universally unique so you will have to make sure your bucket name has not been used before. By "universally," I mean across all AWS regions and accounts. Within the S3 settings while configuring your bucket, you are presented with options such as Versioning, Logging, and Tags. We will leave the default values for now. The only thing we will change is the public permissions. We will make the objects in this bucket open to the public so we can access these recipe images from the web.

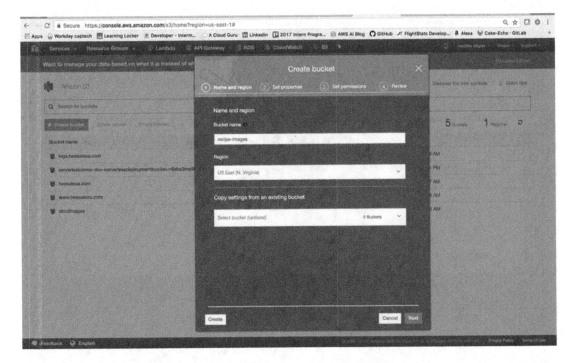

Figure 3-35. *The Create Bucket option lets you configure your blob storage bucket on the fly. You can also adjust these settings after creating the bucket.*

After our bucket and its respective images are configured, we can move on to setting S3 as our trigger and creating our Lambda function.

Using S3 as a Trigger

From the Lambda console, create a Lambda function called `UpdateRecipe`. This Lambda function will receive events from S3 as an object is uploaded (PUT). It will then update the corresponding object's recipe with an image URL. For simplicity, we will name our image uploads with the key to their corresponding recipe. For example, the recipe for Mac & Cheese has an Id of 2. To associate an image URL with that recipe, we will upload a file named 2.

Within the Lambda console, configure your trigger to be S3, and select the bucket that you created previously. Your trigger will end up looking like Figure 3-36.

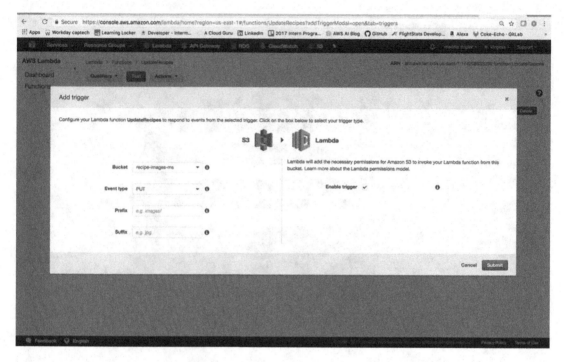

Figure 3-36. *S3 is configured to trigger our Update Lambda on a Put request. This means Lambda will be triggered any time an object is uploaded to the S3 bucket we specified.*

Now that an S3 event is set to trigger our Lambda, we can format our function to handle the event the way we would like it to. The first step is understanding the event request that is coming in. To simulate this request, I used the Set Test Event blueprint for the S3 PUT operation. The following JSON is what it provides:

```
{
 "Records": [
 {
  "eventVersion": "2.0",
  "eventTime": "1970-01-01T00:00:00.000Z",
  "requestParameters": {
  "sourceIPAddress": "127.0.0.1"
 },
  "s3": {
  "configurationId": "testConfigRule",
  "object": {
   "eTag": "0123456789abcdef0123456789abcdef",
   "sequencer": "0A1B2C3D4E5F678901",
   "key": "HappyFace.jpg",
   "size": 1024
 },
  "bucket": {
   "arn": "arn:aws:s3:::mybucket",
   "name": "sourcebucket",
```

```
    "ownerIdentity": {
    "principalId": "EXAMPLE"
    }
    },
    "s3SchemaVersion": "1.0"
    },
    "responseElements": {
    "x-amz-id-2": "EXAMPLE123/5678abcdefghijklambdaisawesome/mnopqrstuvwxyzABCDEFGH",
    "x-amz-request-id": "EXAMPLE123456789"
    },
    "awsRegion": "us-east-1",
    "eventName": "ObjectCreated:Put",
    "userIdentity": {
    "principalId": "EXAMPLE"
    },
    "eventSource": "aws:s3"
  }
  ]
}
```

We can format our Lambda to handle this request by creating a TypeScript model for the S3 PUT request. We want to specify the object key so we can parse it and grab the associated DynamoDB item in order to place the image URL with the correct recipe. The next section will cover how our Lambda function handles this request.

Response to Trigger

As we did with the HTTP request, we will also rely on the AWS SDK to update our DynamoDB table. We want to grab the object key from our incoming event and specify that as our key to the DynamoDB table. Once we have the item we want from our table, we can make changes to it, such as adding an imageUrl attribute and attaching the public URL to the image of the meal.

```
'use strict';
exports.__esModule = true;
var AWS = require("aws-sdk");
module.exports.UpdateRecipe = function (event, context, callback) {
 console.info("Received event: ", JSON.stringify(event, null, 2));
 var docClient = new AWS.DynamoDB.DocumentClient();
 var table = process.env.TABLE_NAME;
 var image = event.Records[0].s3.object.key.split('.');
 var id = parseInt(image[0]);
 // Update the item, unconditionally,
 var params = {
  TableName: table,
  Key: {
   "Id": id
  },
  UpdateExpression: "set ImageURL=:iurl",
  ExpressionAttributeValues: {
   ":iurl": "https://s3.amazonaws.com/recipe-images-ms/" + event.Records[0].s3.object.key
  },
```

```
 ReturnValues: "UPDATED_NEW"
};
var response = {
 statusCode: 200,
 message: ""
};
console.log("Updating the item...");
docClient.update(params, function (err, data) {
 if (err) {
  response.statusCode = 500;
  console.error("Unable to update item. Error JSON:", JSON.stringify(err, null, 2));
  response.message = "Unable to update";
  callback(null, response);
 }
 else {
  console.log("UpdateItem succeeded:", JSON.stringify(data, null, 2));
  response.message = "Updated recipe successfully.";
  callback(null, response);
 }
});
};
```

The following steps summarize this process:

1. Parse the incoming request to gather the key from the image.

2. Set the Image ID to the Key ID to search DynamoDB and find the correct recipe.

3. Your bucket ARN is the beginning of the S3 object image URL. Use this and the name of the image to set the URL in the DynamoDB table.

4. Finally, return the status of the execution.

To test the success of our function after zipping it with the Shared folder and the node modules, we can upload an image to our S3 bucket. I found a picture of mac & cheese, one of my recipes, and uploaded it to the bucket. To upload to the bucket, simply go to the bucket location and click Upload. The prompt is shown in Figure 3-37.

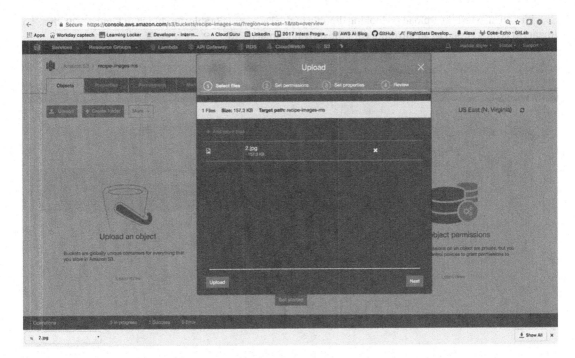

***Figure 3-37.** You can upload the file within the S3 console and configure its permissions on the fly*

Figure 3-38 shows the log results from the upload.

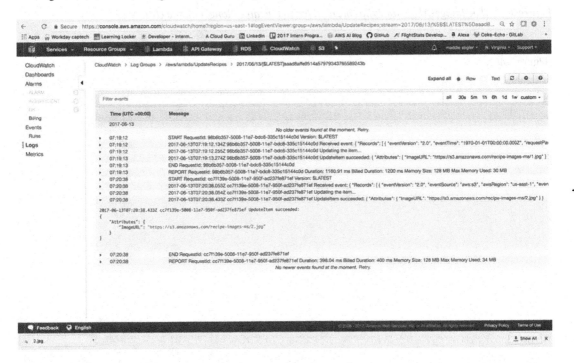

***Figure 3-38.** The successful log results from our upload in CloudWatch*

We can also test the upload by looking directly in the DynamoDB table. As shown in Figure 3-39, the ImageUrl is now added as an attribute with the provided image URL.

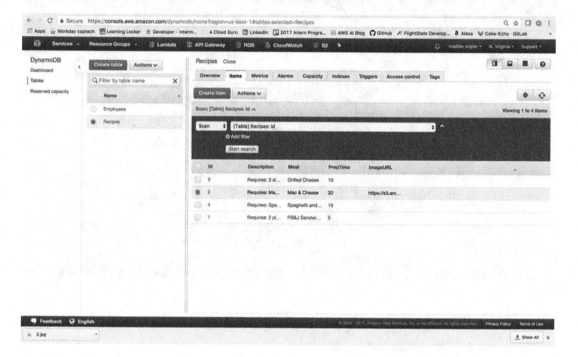

Figure 3-39. *The ImageUrl attribute has been added to the table along with the URL*

Furthermore, when you open the provided image URL, you are redirected to an image of the recipe (Figure 3-40).

Figure 3-40. *The image is publicly accessible with the S3 URL*

As before, there are many ways to improve on this Lambda function. Separation of provider logic is strongly encouraged as well as deploying with the Serverless Framework. The code for this portion of the exercise can be found at https://github.com/mgstigler/Serverless/tree/master/AWS/aws-service/StorageTrigger

Conclusion

In this chapter we explored two serverless applications with AWS Lambda. You learned how to navigate the console, configure Lambda functions, and assign triggers, as well as how to build a couple services to both trigger and respond to Lambda functions. You should now have a good handle on how Lambda functions operate and the power they have within AWS. You should also have a more applicable understanding of serverless functions as a whole and how they can be used. In the next chapter, we will explore the Azure UI and build serverless functions within Azure.

CHAPTER 4

■■■

Azure

In this chapter, we will utilize Azure Functions to create several serverless applications. Previously, we looked at AWS and created two functions, one triggered by an S3 bucket upload and one triggered by an HTTP request. We will recreate these two triggers with different real-world examples using Azure's services. This will give us a look into Azure's resources and how they differ from AWS. It will also allow us to explore other ways to create and use serverless applications. For the following exercises, we will use Azure functions, WebHooks, API triggers, and Azure Queue Storage. By the end of this chapter, we will have three serverless applications and experience with several Azure services as well as a better understanding of picking cloud providers.

■ **Note** We will be looking at different services than we did in AWS to provide exposure to different trigger sources. As further exercise, I recommend going back to Chapter 3 and trying to implement those same solutions using Azure. You could also do the reverse and take the exercises from this chapter and look at them in AWS.

Explore the UI

As we did with AWS, before we begin writing our applications, we will go over the Azure UI and how to navigate it, along with the various pricing options, and the Functions portal. I am someone who started developing in AWS and became very comfortable with the environment and UI that Amazon provides. Ultimately, making the jump from AWS to Azure isn't a tough one, but the interfaces do vary a bit, and that can be a little tricky to get used to. To help ease this difference, I'll walk through it pointing out various comparisons and differences between the two. To get to the Azure portal, go to `http://www.portal.azure.com`. After signing in, you will be directed to your dashboard. The dashboard gives you an overview of your resources, some tips and tricks, and your running services. Figure 4-1 demonstrates an example Dashboard.

© Maddie Stigler 2018

M. Stigler, *Beginning Serverless Computing*, https://doi.org/10.1007/978-1-4842-3084-8_4

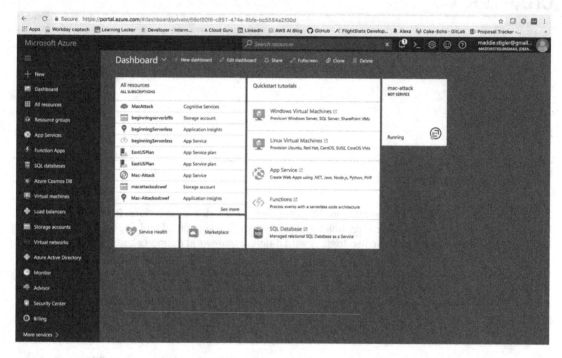

Figure 4-1. *Azure gives you an overview of your resources and running services. It also gives you access to creating new resources on the left panel.*

Something that I really enjoy about the Azure dashboard is its ability to be customized. By clicking the Edit Dashboard option at the top, you can easily add other resources, move resources, and add tiles. A *tile* is simply a single block on your dashboard (examples include All Resources, Service Health, and Marketplace in Figure 4-1). The Tile Gallery is a tool that allows you to search for tiles for a particular resource and drag them onto your current blade (as you'll see shortly, a UI to specific resources). Through this, you are able to make management views spanning resources. You also have the ability to create and view multiple dashboards. I like to use different dashboards for different projects so I can keep all of my resources visually separated. You can give each dashboard a project name to keep organized.

■ **Note**   It is important to keep in mind that the UI in Azure changes quite often, possibly even more so than other providers. It would not be uncommon to log in one day and see a different UI or items with changed names.

Navigation

We've explored a lot of the capabilities of the dashboard, but there are many other points of interest straight on the portal page that will benefit us to understand early on. As in AWS, there is a bell icon on the top black bar that gives us any service updates from Azure. Next to the bell, we have the Cloud Shell. This is a feature that I really love, so I will spend some time going over it. Figure 4-2 shows the startup screen of the Cloud Shell.

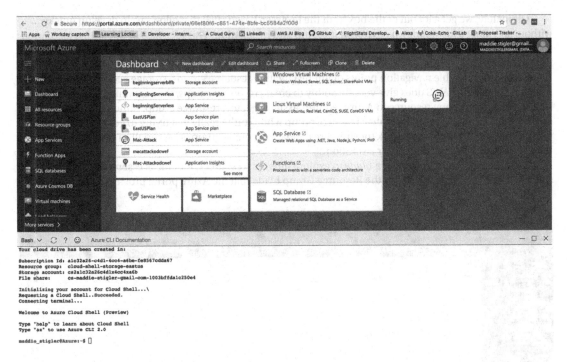

Figure 4-2. *When you click the Cloud Shell icon, Azure pulls up a Bash Shell that comes with the Azure CLI and many other features.*

As of now, you can use the Shell to execute Bash commands or switch it to a PowerShell preview. I suspect the PowerShell option will be coming out pretty soon, but for now, the preview will do. By typing in **az**, you get the full Azure CLI. This is an incredible feature. The ability to grab the CLI in one command straight from the portal makes things so much easier. To me, this takes a step even further away from relying on anything locally and further places it in the cloud provider's location. This is something you will probably notice with Azure as we move forward; Microsoft has done a great job of removing as much from the local workspace as possible. I predict this will continue to be a trend and will be something that other cloud providers, such as AWS and Google, catch up on.

■ **Note**   Azure shell sessions aren't persistent, but your data will be stored between sessions. In addition, sessions are automatically synced to a $Home directory that now allows you to save files and scripts for reuse. This also means you can now use vi right from the Azure portal.

Azure provides us a list of some things to keep in mind when using the Azure Cloud Shell:

- Cloud Shell times out after 10 minutes without interactive activity.

- Cloud Shell can only be accessed with a file share attached.

- Cloud Shell is assigned one machine per user account.

- Permissions are set as a regular Linux user.

- Cloud Shell runs on a temporary machine provided on a per-session, per-user basis.

Ultimately, we get a lot out of the box from the browser-based shell that allows us to develop quickly without spending a lot of time on environment setup and installation. This idea falls in line with a lot of what serverless computing is. Cloud providers are here to ease the development process by providing as much off the bat as they can.

Some other notable navigation points of interest include resource groups, storage accounts, billing, and function apps. While AWS does give you the ability to create resource groups, they are much less enforced. By contrast, creating any resource in Azure requires assigning it to a resource group. Although sometimes it can be a bit of a pain to have to create a resource group while you're really just trying to get your application up and running, I have to say I think they're a great idea. A resource group is essentially a container used to hold all of your related resources for a solution.

Azure also uses the concept of a *blade* to explore different resources. A blade is essentially a UI for a specific resource. Figure 4-3 shows the Resource Group blade that the Azure portal provides.

Figure 4-3. *The Resource Groups blade allows you to view all of your resource groups, create another resource group, and organize your current groups.*

In this portal, I have a resource group for beginning serverless, which contains all of my resources for our first serverless example, our cloud shell storage (this is required to use the Cloud Shell), and then a couple of bot storage groups. You can also give different resource groups different tags to sort them even more generally. Some people use this as a way to keep different development environments separate. An example of this would be creating resource groups for your different solutions and tagging them as Dev, QA, Production, or whatever you choose. You can then filter them in the future by specific development environment.

The Storage Account resource (Figure 4-4) is another Azure service that you will be accessing frequently while using Azure as your cloud provider. Similar to resource groups, most Azure services require you to assign them to a storage group. In my experience, this actually simplifies things later on because you know exactly where everything is ending up and how to monitor and configure it. One of the tricky aspects of AWS is that Amazon handles a lot of this setup for you, and if you are unfamiliar with the provisioning and configuration, there could be seemingly random security groups and settings that aren't as obvious to find. By creating these elements specifically for your resource group, you know exactly where to go to make any configuration changes.

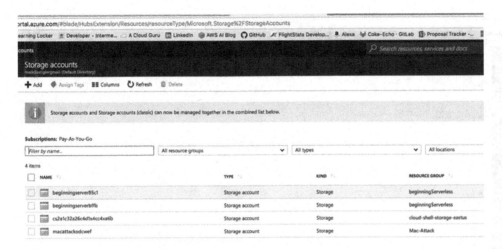

Figure 4-4. *The Storage Accounts Blade lets you view all of your storage groups and the resource groups associated with them*

As you can see, I have a storage account associated with each of my resource groups viewed earlier. All of the objects in a storage account are billed together. Azure recommends you keep the following in mind when creating storage accounts:

- Account type refers to whether you are using a general-purpose storage account or a Blob storage account. With a Blob storage account, the access tier also determines the billing model for the account.

- Storage capacity refers to how much of your storage account allotment you are using to store data.

- Replication determines how many copies of your data are maintained at one time, and in what locations. It is also important to note that pricing is different for some of these replication options. It is worth looking into before making the decision and getting a bill you aren't expecting.

- Transactions refer to all read and write operations to Azure Storage.

- Data egress refers to data transferred out of an Azure region. When the data in your storage account is accessed by an application that is not running in the same region, you are charged for data egress. (For Azure services, you can take steps to group your data and services in the same data centers to reduce or eliminate data egress charges).

- The region refers to the geographical region in which your account is based.

Service Accounts for specific accounts give you options including viewing the services included in the account, adding access keys, providing metrics on your resources, and gives you access to services such as Tables, Queues, Blob Storage, and Azure VMs. Figure 4-5 gives you an overview of all of these options.

Figure 4-5. *The Storage Accounts Blade also gives you insight into particular storage accounts with various actions and metrics on the account itself*

You are also given storage account endpoints to be able to easily and quickly access the resources in your storage account. Each URL address is unique to the object stored in Azure Storage. The account name forms the subdomain of that address, so the combination of the subdomain and domain name forms the endpoint for your storage account. For example, my beginning serverless resource group is under the storage account `beginningserverbffb`.

- Blob service: `http://beginningserverbffb.blob.core.windows.net`

- Table Service: `http://beginningserverbffb.table.core.windows.net`

- File Service: `http://beginningserverbffb.file.core.windows.net`

- Queue Service: `http://beginningserverbffb.queue.core.windows.net`

In addition to storage and resources, we will also look at how to access pricing and billing from the Azure portal.

Pricing

From the Billing blade (Figure 4-6), we have access to very general billing information such as invoices, payment methods, and subscriptions.

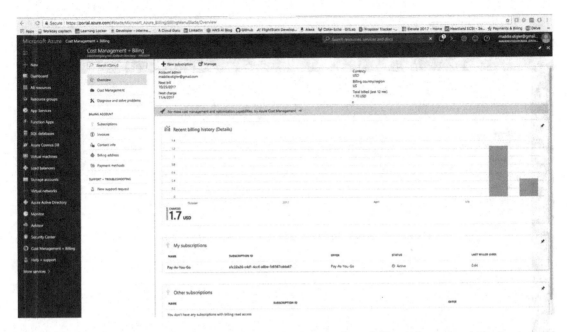

Figure 4-6. *Your Billing blade gives you a very general overview of your billing information and subscription information*

I personally prefer the Billing portal in AWS to Azure, mostly because of the accessibility and ease of use compared to the actual functionality. In AWS, we were able to do everything in our billing management from the same portal. In Azure, you are given a very basic overview and are required to go to the actual Azure account page (in a different portal) to manage your account billing.

Another difference is that in Azure, you can set billing limits and have your items stopped if they hit that limit. This is different than in AWS where you can only set a billing alarm.

From the actual subscription in your billing, you can view different metrics such as cost by resource, cost analysis, and usage. You can also control IAM, transferring of subscriptions, and the resources associated with the particular subscription.

Azure Functions

The Azure Function Apps are accessible from the side Resources panel. When you open it, you are directed to the Functions blade. This blade shows all of your function apps and the project structures of each. Figure 4-7 demonstrates the Functions blade.

Figure 4-7. *The Function Apps blade with all of your functions and project structure*

I was reluctant to embrace Azure functions because I had done so much development with AWS Lambda and cloud development within the AWS sphere. However, after navigating around Functions for a little bit, I quickly became a huge fan. One of my qualms about AWS Lambda was the inability to view and navigate project structure efficiently. Azure solved this problem by giving you a way to access your project structure, easily make changes and configure your serverless applications, and do all of this in one spot.

I do think this is something that will be available with AWS as it continues to grow. For now, it is an incredibly helpful feature within Azure functions and something that should make rapid development even quicker. Azure also incorporates the idea of *inputs* and *outputs*, which can be configured from the Integrate blade in your particular function. We discussed inputs and outputs briefly, but they basically just allow you to bind additional data to your function (such as retrieving from a table) as they are triggered. Figure 4-8 shows the project structure of a simple Hello World function we will be exploring later.

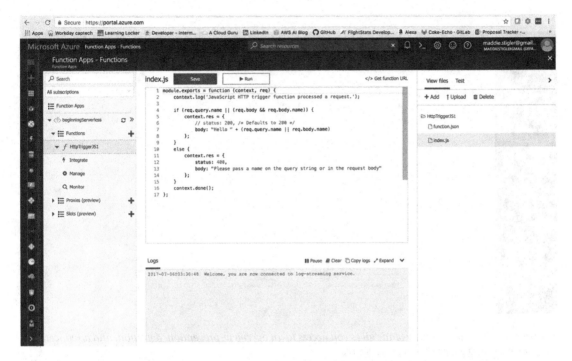

Figure 4-8. The Azure Function Apps lets you view your function based on its configuration, as seen on the left. It also lets you view your function's project structure and edit the various files contained within it.

We will explore the Function Apps and all of their capabilities in more detail as we begin creating our solutions. However, before we can get started creating our functions, we should look at Azure security. We did this with AWS as well when looking into IAM. It is good practice to have a good understanding of each provider's security capabilities so you can create secure yet accessible applications. Azure helps you out more than you expect by requiring you to associate all of your resources with an application. This leads to better organization and less confusion when configuring permissions. I tend to get a little confused when I have a lot of roles and different permissions, so creating it from the start and knowing it is specific to the exact resource I am creating helps me out a lot.

Azure Security

We can navigate to Azure Security by clicking on the Hamburger and going to More Services and Security Center. The Security Center will look something like the dashboard in Figure 4-9.

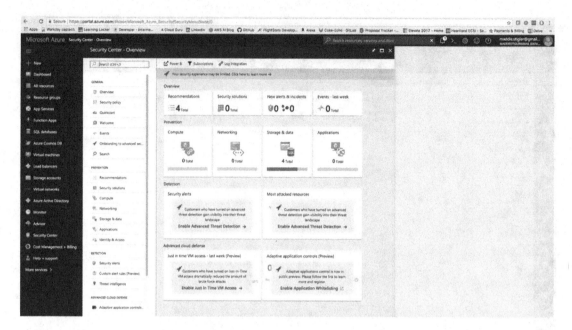

Figure 4-9. *The Azure Security blade gives you access to an overview, prevention, detection, and advanced cloud defense with your account and services*

The Azure Security Center helps you prevent, detect, and respond to threats with increased visibility into and control over the security of your Azure resources. It provides integrated security monitoring and policy management across your Azure subscriptions, helps detect threats that might otherwise go unnoticed, and works with a broad ecosystem of security solutions. Microsoft lists several key capabilities:

Azure Security Stages

Stage	Capability
Prevent	Monitors the security state of your Azure resources.
Prevent	Defines policies for your Azure subscriptions based on your company's security requirements, the types of applications that you use, and the sensitivity of your data.
Prevent	Uses policy-driven security recommendations to guide service owners through the process of implementing needed controls.
Prevent	Rapidly deploys security services and appliances from Microsoft and partners.
Detect	Automatically collects and analyzes security data from your Azure resources, the network, and partner solutions like antimalware programs and firewalls.
Detect	Uses global threat intelligence from Microsoft products and services, the Microsoft Digital Crimes Unit (DCU), the Microsoft Security Response Center (MSRC), and external feeds.
Detect	Applies advanced analytics, including machine learning and behavioral analysis.
Respond	Provides prioritized security incidents/alerts.
Respond	Offers insights into the source of the attack and impacted resources.
Respond	Suggests ways to stop the current attack and help prevent future attacks.

You can access these capabilities from the Security Center in the portal.

Implement Recommendations

Security Center periodically analyzes the security state of your Azure resources. When Security Center identifies potential security vulnerabilities, it creates recommendations that guide you through the process of configuring the needed controls.

These recommendations provided by Azure are something you should check routinely. I went back after creating my applications for this chapter and implemented the security recommendations from the Security Center. Figure 4-10 shows what my recommendations were and how you can easily find them on the blade.

Figure 4-10. *The Azure Security blade gives you access to an overview, prevention, detection, and advanced cloud defense with your account and services*

The recommendations are shown in a table format where each line represents one particular recommendation. The columns of this table are:

DESCRIPTION: Explains the recommendation and what needs to be done to address it.

RESOURCE: Lists the resources to which this recommendation applies.

STATE: Describes the current state of the recommendation:

Open: The recommendation hasn't been addressed yet.

In Progress: The recommendation is currently being applied to the resources, and no action is required by you.

Resolved: The recommendation has already been completed (in this case, the line is grayed out).

SEVERITY: Describes the severity of that particular recommendation:

High: A vulnerability exists with a meaningful resource (such as an application, a VM, or a network security group) and requires attention.

Medium: A vulnerability exists and noncritical or additional steps are required to eliminate it or to complete a process.

Low: A vulnerability exists that should be addressed but does not require immediate attention. (By default, low recommendations aren't presented, but you can filter on low recommendations if you want to see them.)

Some of my recommendations came from my Pay-As-You-Go plan. Azure wants you to use the Standard plan, which is a bit pricier. For the sake of this project, you can stick to the free tier and then shift up as you start needing more from your plan.

Set Security Policies

The last thing I want to look at in the Security Center before jumping into our function is the security policies. A security policy defines the set of controls that are recommended for resources within the specified subscription. In Security Center, you define policies for your Azure subscriptions according to your company/personal security needs and the type of applications or sensitivity of the data in each subscription.

For example, resources that are used for development or testing might have different security requirements from resources that are used for production applications. I am currently developing an application for my client in AWS and we are also using policies and different accounts to set up different resources for different development environments. Likewise, applications that use regulated data like personally identifiable information might require a higher level of security. Security policies that are enabled in Azure Security Center drive security recommendations and monitoring to help you identify potential vulnerabilities and mitigate threats. If you are developing for a company based on its security needs, I recommend reading Azure Security Center Planning and Operations Guide: https://docs.microsoft.com/en-us/azure/security-center/security-center-planning-and-operations-guide.

We can configure security policies for each subscription. Start by clicking the Policy tile in the Security Center dashboard (Figure 4-11).

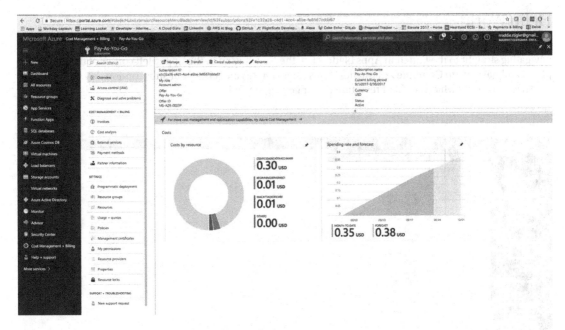

Figure 4-11. *The Policies for each subscription are available in the Security Center dashboard*

In this blade, we can edit security policies by clicking on the subscription we want to edit. The available options for each subscription include these:

- **Prevention policy**: Use this option to configure policies per subscription.

- **Email notification**: Use this option to configure an email notification that's sent on the first daily occurrence of an alert and for high severity alerts. Email preferences can be configured only for subscription policies.

- **Pricing tier**: Use this option to upgrade the pricing tier selection.

- **Security Policy**: In this blade, click Prevention Policy to see the available options. Click On to enable the security recommendations that are relevant for this subscription.

Since we are using functions for our serverless application, we will not need to edit much in the Security Policies section. However, is the options here are good to know moving forward, so when you start incorporating different services in your application you'll know where to set the security policies.

Your First Code

In this section, we are going to cover the basics to setting up a Hello World function, similar to the one we created in AWS. It's important to redo these steps with a small function first because while you get a lot of the same out of the box, each provider is very different and the setup can be different, too.

Hello World

We are going to start by creating our Hello World function through the Azure portal. To begin, instead of navigating straight to the Function Apps blade, click the New button in the upper-left corner of the Azure portal and navigate to Compute ➤ Function Apps (Figure 4-12) and click your subscription. My subscription is a "pay as you go," which is what I recommend for getting started.

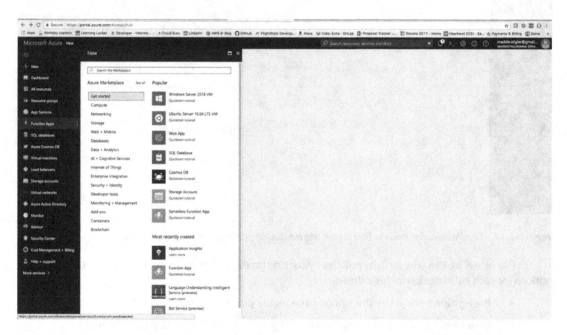

Figure 4-12. *We are going to create a new Azure Function through the Function App option in the New resource blade*

You will need to fill out a couple of things to create your hello world function including the App Name, Subscription, Resource Group, Hosting Plan, Location, Storage, and yes or no to Application Insights. I've listed some helpful hints that Microsoft gives you regarding filling out these various fields:

- **App Name:** Globally unique.

- **Resource Group:** Name of the resource group to create your app in.

- **Hosting Plan:** Defines how resources are allocated to your app. In the default, resources are added dynamically as required by your functions. You only pay for the time your functions run.

- **Location:** Choose one near to where your services will run.

- **Storage Account:** Also globally unique, name of the new or existing storage account.

Figure 4-13 shows the final settings for my serverless function app.

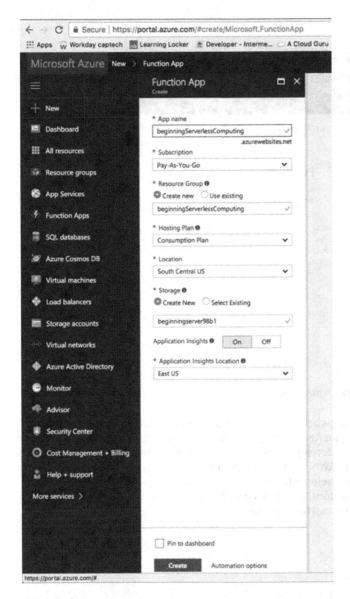

Figure 4-13. I put my Hello World function in my region and created a resource group of the same name

---

■ **Note**   It is important to remember that your app name and your storage account must be globally unique. You will not be able to name them the same as mine, so pick something that still defines what you are building.

I chose to pin the function to my dashboard to make it easily accessible moving forward. Once you are ready to go, click Create to create and initialize your Hello World function. When you click Create, Azure will take you back to the portal while the function is being created (Figure 4-14). If you chose to save it to your dashboard, you will see the App's creation progress directly on your dashboard. If you didn't, you can still view the progress by clicking on the bell in the top-right corner of the portal.

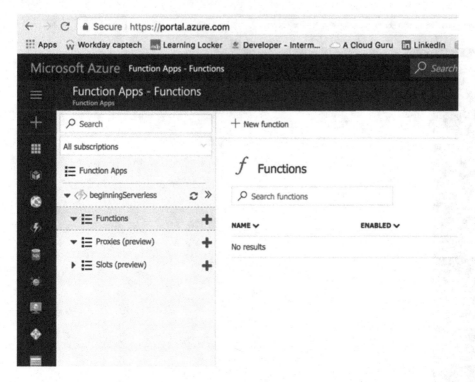

Figure 4-14. *Notice that the project has been created, but there are no functions listed underneath it*

In Azure, we create larger resources groups before creating the actual resource. In AWS, we created the function directly. AWS requires fewer steps, but Azure gives you slightly more organization and allows you to look at it as you are accustomed to doing as a developer. This method also lets you keep all of your functions associated with the same project together. In AWS, it can get a little hectic trying to keep all of a project's functions together. It is really up to what you prefer as the architect.

When we click the plus icon next to functions, we are taken to the startup page, which gives you three out-of-the-box templates for creating a function. These options are:

- WebHooks and API
- Timer
- Data Processing

You are also given three runtime options:

- FSharp
- CSharp
- JavaScript

We are going to select the WebHooks and API template so we can build off it later for our next function. Azure actually gives you even more templating options than this if you click on Create Custom Function. To me, this option name is a little misleading. These templates all already have triggers configured for each runtime and each trigger option. In AWS, you are given far more template options to start out with, as well as other runtimes. This gives you a little more flexibility as the developer. Azure also lets you create your own custom function both in PowerShell and from the console. We are going to select the JavaScript runtime and create our function. Figure 4-15 shows what your new function in our Hello World project should look like.

Figure 4-15. The recently created function using the Webhook + API template

As you can see, we really do get a lot out of the box with this template. We now have a function under our Functions option in our project. If we click on the function itself, we can see and edit the index.js file to do what we want. Right now, the function takes a POST request with a name object and returns a string saying "Hello {Name}". By clicking Integrate in the function options, we can see the trigger configuration for the HTTP request (Figure 4-16).

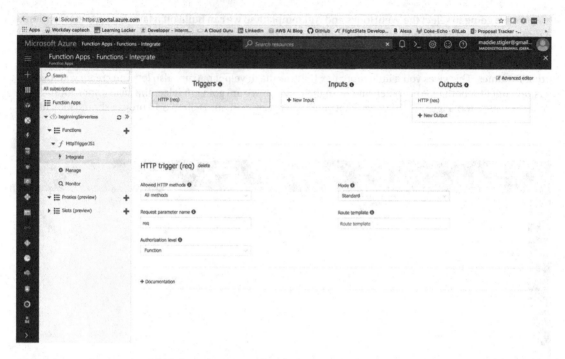

Figure 4-16. *The Integrate blade lets you view the trigger (a mandatory feature of the Azure function), configure inputs and outputs, and advanced HTTP features*

In the HTTP Trigger section, we are given the following options:

- **Allowed HTTP Methods**: Configurable.

- **Request Parameter Name**: The name used to identify this trigger in the code.

- **Authorization Level**: Controls whether the function requires an API key and which key to use:

- **Mode**: Standard or WebHook.

- **Route Template**: Allows you to change the URI that triggers the function.

For those of you who prefer to configure this manually, you can use the Advanced Editor in the top right corner to edit the function.json file. This file determines the bindings and settings of the function trigger. To begin, I thought it was easier to configure using the UI, but as I became more comfortable, I enjoyed making these changes in the Advanced Editor because it became quicker.

In the Manage section under our function, you are given options to edit Function State, Function Keys, and Host Keys (Figure 4-17).

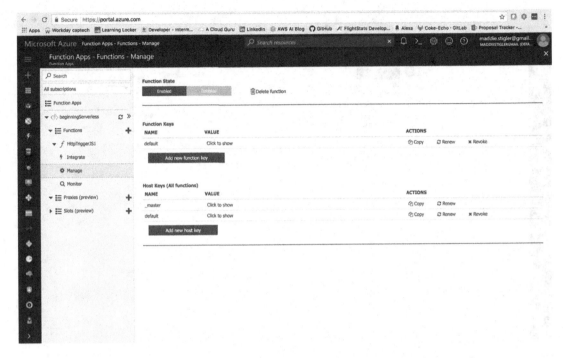

Figure 4-17. *The Manage blade is where your keys and state can be configured and managed*

You can use these keys as a query parameter in your requests. If your function is a WebHook (as opposed to a regular HTTP function), when using a key other than the default you must also specify the clientId as a query parameter (the client ID is the name of your new key). We will look at this in more detail later as we build our function out. Now, we are going to jump into testing our function and seeing what it comes with right out of the template.

Testing

To test our Hello World HTTP function, we are simply going to click back on the function name, and open the Test blade on the right side of the portal. As you can see, the test options are provided for us to configure and send through. The test options are already configured for your specific trigger, so we can see HTTP request options including method, query, header, and request body.

For our function, all we need to kick things off is a request body with a name. I'm going to pass my own name in as the request (Figure 4-18).

Figure 4-18. *The sample test event with my name being passed into the request. Azure gives you the output and the logs as soon as the request is complete.*

The output and logs resemble AWS and are pretty easy to follow. Azure gives you a couple of extra options for the logs including Pause, Clear, Copy, and Expand. Azure also provides all of the monitoring for the function execution in the function blade. To monitor these logs closely, we will navigate to the Monitor blade underneath our function. Here we are given the success count, error count, and the invocation log with invocation details (Figure 4-19).

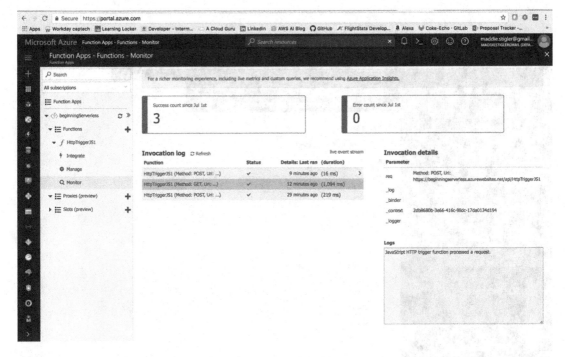

Figure 4-19. *This figure shows the Monitor blade under the function we are testing and everything you get from that blade*

While this does provide us with the monitoring we need for a Hello World project, we are going to go ahead and look into Application Insights, setting it up, and what we can learn from it.

Application Insights

Application Insights (Figure 4-20) is a powerful metrics tool that takes little effort to set up and associate with your function. Azure recommends developers utilize Application Insights with all of their functions. To get started, click the New button on the resources panel and choose Developer Tools ➤ Application Insights.

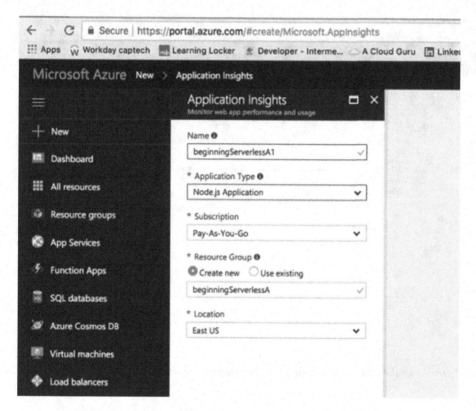

Figure 4-20. *Application Insights configuration for my beginning serverless function. Note that I put it in the same resource group I had created earlier.*

Once you create your Application Insights, grab the Instrumentation Key from the Essentials and copy it. This key will be used to link our function to the Insights instance. From here, navigate back to your Hello World function. Click on your project ➤ Settings ➤ Manage Application Settings. Under App Settings (Figure 4-21), locate APPINSIGHTS_INSTRUMENTATIONKEY and paste your key into the box next to it. Save these changes. This will tell App Insights what to watch and monitor. As soon as the key is associated with your function, your application will start sending App Insights monitoring information about your function without any other configuration.

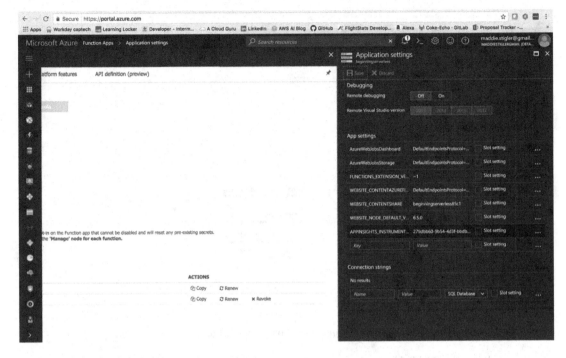

Figure 4-21. *This figure demonstrates how to add your App Insights Key to your function*

Application Insights is a great tool not only because of its ease of use, but also for its extensibility. This service spans many platforms including .NET, Node.js, and J2EE. Azure is currently the only provider to support .NET Core for application monitoring. It can also be used on premises or in the cloud. I recently started using Application Insights at my client site with an on-premises application, and it is just as simple to use. It also integrates well with other cloud services and has several connection points to different development tools, including these:

- Azure Diagnostics
- Docker logs
- PowerBI
- REST API
- Continuous Export

These tools can be used to measure your Application Insights. Within Azure, Application Insights can be explored much more easily. Azure provides a built-in dashboard that allows you to explore all of your insights for your function and export these insights. To experience the full extent of Application Insights, navigate to the new resource we created in the dashboard (Figure 4-22).

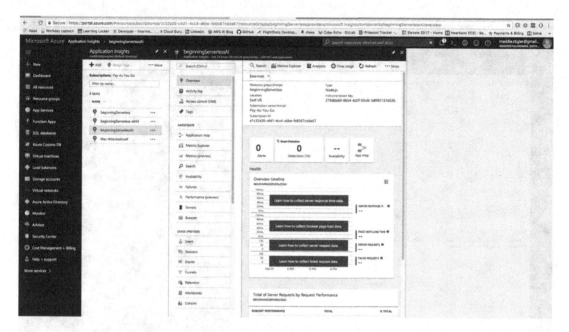

Figure 4-22. *Application Insights Blade for our Hello World Application*

By just clicking on the blade, you are given a lot up front including alerts, availability, app map, health, and total requests. These give you a good overview of your function, but a lot of the power of Application Insights remains to be seen. By going to the Analytics tab, you are redirected to an Application Insights page that gives you everything you need to continue monitoring your application. Microsoft provides these additional features as well:

- **Request rates, response times, and failure rates:** Find out which pages are most popular, at what times of day, and where your users are. See which pages perform best. If your response times and failure rates go high when there are more requests, then perhaps you have a resourcing problem.

- **Dependency rates, response times, and failure rates:** Find out whether external services are slowing you down.

- **Exceptions:** Analyze the aggregated statistics, or pick specific instances and drill into the stack trace and related requests. Both server and browser exceptions are reported.

- **Page views and load performance:** Reported by your users' browsers.

- **AJAX calls from web pages:** Rates, response times, and failure rates.

- **Performance counters** from your Windows or Linux server machines, such as CPU, memory, and network usage.

- **Host diagnostics** from Docker or Azure.

- **Diagnostic trace logs** from your app — so that you can correlate trace events with requests.

- **Custom events and metrics** that you write yourself in the client or server code, to track business events such as items sold or games won.

HTTP Events

We are going to look at HTTP events in two parts: WebHooks as a trigger and API as a trigger. For our first built-out Azure function, we will build a simple WebHook application. In our second one, we will build off our Hello World function. I wanted to explore WebHooks because this is a feature Azure provides to users and it departs from AWS resources a bit. Before beginning, it is important to understand the concept of a WebHook. I tend to like to jump into projects and get my hands dirty so I didn't spend as much time understanding WebHooks as I should have. After several failed attempts, I finally took the time to really research WebHooks and how they function.

A WebHook is simply a method of changing the behavior of a web application or web page with custom callbacks. Callbacks are a significant concept in most applications and especially so in Node.js applications. To put it simply, callbacks are functions passed to functions that signify the end of a specific task. In Node. js, callbacks are especially necessary due to the asynchronous nature of Node. This means functions can execute in parallel. In cases where order matters, it is important to include a callback to indicate the end of a function. Figure 4-23 illustrates the idea of a callback in Node.

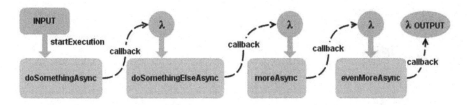

Figure 4-23. *Callbacks signifying the end of a function and the start of another function*

Since callbacks are a pretty significant topic in event-driven applications and serverless applications tend to be event-driven, I would recommend researching this topic in further detail if it is not understood. I really liked this article at tutorialspoint: `https://www.tutorialspoint.com/nodejs/nodejs_callbacks_concept.htm`. I had a hard time implementing callbacks (I would frequently leave them out when I first started writing applications in Node), and this tutorial helped me understand their use.

The custom callbacks we will use for our WebHook will be maintained, modified, and managed by GitHub. For the purpose of this exercise, we are going to use a GitHub-triggered WebHook to gain a better understanding of how we can utilize WebHooks in our Azure functions and how we can use third-party sources (GitHub) to configure them.

Create a GitHub WebHook Trigger

In our Azure Functions blade, we are going to create a new function and pick the GitHub WebHook – JavaScript template provided by the Azure library (Figure 4-24). The starter template for this will provide us with a function URL and a GitHub secret that we will use to link our GitHub account to our Azure function.

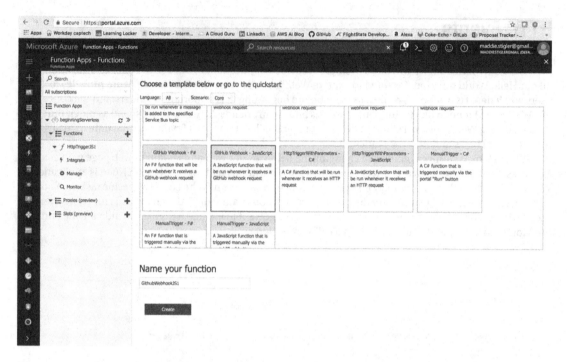

Figure 4-24. *Select the GitHub WebHook Template from the Azure library*

By clicking the function URL and the GitHub Secret, we can collect the information needed to configure the WebHook in GitHub. As it is, the function is triggered by an action, to be decided, that is coming from our GitHub account. I am using my personal GitHub account to trigger this function (Figure 4-25). If you do not have an account, go ahead and sign up for a free one at `http://www.github.com`. If you do not already have a repository, feel free to fork mine at `https://github.com/mgstigler/Serverless/tree/master/Azure/azure-service`.

CHAPTER 4 ■ AZURE

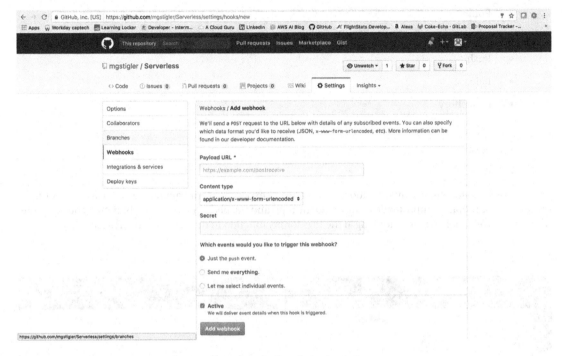

Figure 4-25. *Paste the URL and Secret in your Github WebHooks settings*

If you navigate to the settings of your repo, you will see a WebHooks tab where you can paste your Payload URL and Secret. Leave the content type as `application/x-www-form-urlencoded`. You can specify which events you would like to trigger the WebHook, from the following list:

- Commit comment

- Create

- Deployment

- Fork

- Gollum

- Issue comment

- Issues

- Label

- Member

- Milestone

- Page build

- Project

- Project card

- Project column

- Public

- Pull request

- Push

- Release

- Repository

- Status

- Team add

- Watch

I chose a push event for my WebHook, but feel free to experiment with anything you wish. After setting up this configuration, I simply made a change to my repo and pushed it to my master branch. I could see the effect of the WebHook trigger by looking at the logs for my function in the Azure portal (Figure 4-26).

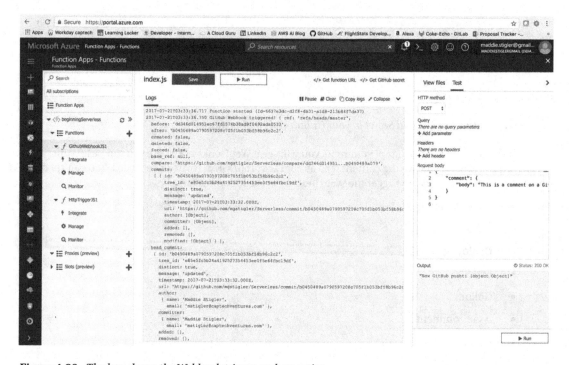

Figure 4-26. *The logs shows the Webhook trigger and execution*

My function's body simply writes the request to the logs. You can see everything about the push to my repo, including the committer, timestamp, and what I changed. This may not be so helpful right now, but you can see how WebHooks could be used to set up GitHub apps that subscribe to various events on GitHub. These applications can be used to update an issue tracker, trigger continuous integration builds, and even deploy to different environments. This example wraps up our GitHub WebHook example. If you are interested in learning more, I found this to be a good resource: `https://developer.github.com/webhooks/`.

Build Upon Our Hello World API Trigger

To build on our HTTP trigger, we are going to create a notification service that utilizes Twilio and the Hello World API trigger, as well as Output bindings. I'm going to make this service fun and say it will be a food delivery notification service, but you can make it whatever you like. To create this, we are going to go back to our Hello World function and change the HTTP request from "any" to POST. I like to separate my API calls into different functions. Since the goal of delivering a serverless solution is fast, event-oriented design, we will stick to this approach. To begin, we will reconfigure our function so navigate back to your Hello World. Do the following to reconfigure:

- In Integrate, navigate to Triggers. Change your allowed methods to Selected Methods and choose the POST method. I set my route template to be orders/. Feel free to do the same.

- In Outputs, click Add new Output and choose Twilio from the available outputs.

  - For Message Parameter Name, choose to use the function return value (you can also set your own parameter name if you wish

  - I left the Twilio Settings as TwilioAuthToken and TwilioAccountSid.

  - I also left the rest of the parameters blank so I can configure them in my function.

We are set up in our Azure portal, but now we need a Twilio account and the information associated with that account. To get this information, go to `https://www.twilio.com/try-twilio` and sign up for free. Once you do this, you will reach the Twilio landing page (Figure 4-27), which gives you your Auth Token and Account Sid.

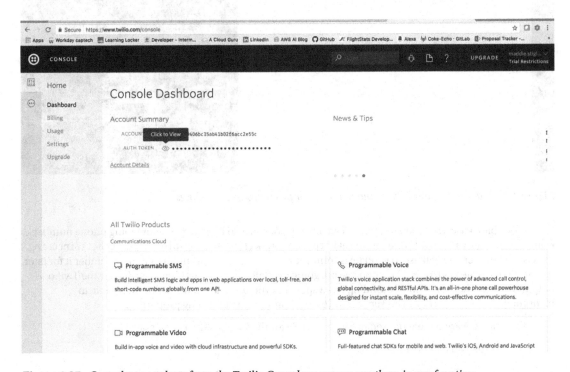

Figure 4-27. *Copy the two tokens from the Twilio Console so we can use them in our function*

I'm going to break here for a Twilio plug. Twilio is a unique developer platform for communication. Developers utilize the Twilio API to add voice, messaging, and video capabilities to their applications. By doing this, they are able to provide the right communications experience to their customers easily and cheaply. Twilio operates by providing a software layer that connects and optimizes communication networks around the world. This is how developers can enable users to reliably call and message anyone anywhere with little to no cost. Current companies utilizing the Twilio API include Uber, Lyft, and Netflix.

While I am someone who enjoys building my own services within cloud environments, I also highly suggest looking into public APIs such as Twilio when necessary. The AWS equivalent to using Twilio is SNS, Simple Notification Service. Both tools can make your life a lot easier and give you a lot more security and reliability than what you would expect.

After you grab your tokens from Twilio, save them in your Application Settings. I saved mine as TwilioAuthToken and TwilioAccountSid (Figure 4-28). You can name them whatever you like, but you will need to configure this in your function outputs.

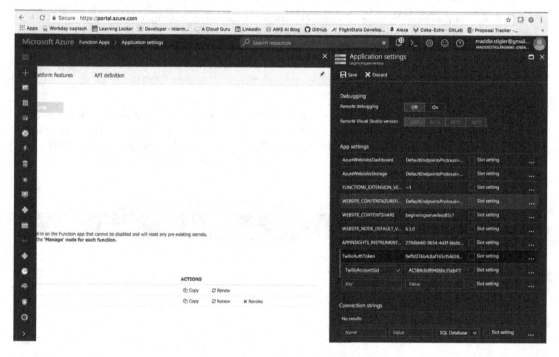

Figure 4-28. *Save the Twilio Tokens and Sid in your app environment settings*

To be able to use the Twilio integration effectively, we will also need to get an outgoing phone number from Twilio. They will provide one for free at https://www.twilio.com/console/phone-numbers/incoming. This is the number you will use to send texts from your function. Store this number and remember it for later.

If you navigate back to our function, we are going to configure the function.json file for the Twilio output binding. The Twilio output binding has a specific structure that we will follow to be able to incorporate it in our function. The function.json will provide the following properties:

> name: Variable name used in function code for the Twilio SMS text message.

> type: Must be set to twilioSms.

accountSid: This value must be set to the name of an App Setting that holds your Twilio Account Sid.

authToken: This value must be set to the name of an App Setting that holds your Twilio authentication token.

to: This value is set to the phone number that the SMS text is sent to.

from: This value is set to the phone number that the SMS text is sent from.

direction: Must be set to out.

body : This value can be used to hard-code the SMS text message if you don't need to set it dynamically in the code for your function.

My final function.json file looks like this:

```
{
 "bindings": [
  {
   "authLevel": "function",
   "type": "httpTrigger",
   "direction": "in",
   "name": "req",
   "route": "orders/",
   "methods": [
    "post"
   ]
  },
  {
   "type": "http",
   "direction": "out",
   "name": "res"
  },
  {
   "type": "twilioSms",
   "name": "$return",
   "accountSid": "TwilioAccountSid",
   "authToken": "TwilioAuthToken",
   "direction": "out"
  }
 ],
 "disabled": false
}
```

At this point, we should have all of the setup done so we can actually write the function. To start, we will need to require Twilio so we can use the Twilio client to send the message. From there, we will simply take the data we are receiving, parse it, and send it in the message. The body of your index.js file should look something like Listing 4-1.

Listing 4-1. Body of the index.js file for our Twilio function

```
var client = require('twilio')(process.env.TwilioAccountSid, process.env.TwilioAuthToken);

module.exports = function (context, req) {
  console.log(req.body.name);
  if(req.body.name && req.body.phoneNumber){
    client.messages.create({
      from: '+18178544390',
      to: req.body.phoneNumber,
      body: "Hello " + req.body.name + "! Your order of " + req.body.order + " is on the way."
    }, function(err, message) {
      if(err) {
        console.error(err.message);
      }
    });
  }

  else {
    console.error("Please include a request body with a name and a phone number");
  }
};
```

We will also need a package.json file since we are using Node modules. Once we have fleshed this out, the trickiest part is actually uploading it to Azure. This is where Azure gets a little tricky. You can't directly upload entire folders from the console. This means you either have to select all of the files one by one before uploading, or you use a framework like Serverless to help you upload (my recommendation), or you use Azure's online command-line tool. I am going to walk through option three so we get some exposure to this. In practice, however, I would definitely use Serverless. I am hoping this is something that changes in the future. The hardest part should not be uploading your project, but it actually is a little exhausting.

Once you have your index, function, and package.json files in your project in the console, navigate to <*functionname*>.scm.azurewebsites.net. This is your function's URL with Kudu. To give a bit of background, Kudu is a deployment framework that can be triggered by Git. It is actually very similar to Visual Studio Online. I used VSOnline at my client site and saw a lot of parallels between that and Kudu when I first started using Kudu. You can check in the code, create a build definition that will build and run the code and tests, and then proceed to push the content to Azure websites.

Another benefit to Kudu, which we will see, is the ability to have more access to and control over your code online. One of my biggest frustrations when I first started working with Azure was not having control over my project. I spent a lot of time looking up solutions to uploading node modules and trying to physically upload them through the Cloud Shell to no avail. I even emailed a mentor and asked how he was able to use node modules with Azure functions; his response was that he never was able to and switched to an entirely different runtime just to avoid the headache.

When I finally found the solution online, it was to use Kudu to interact with your code directly. We are going to do this now so we have a better understanding of both, how to navigate and access your code in the cloud and the benefits of Kudu.

When you first get to your site, you will just see the dashboard. We will go into the Debug console (Figure 4-30) to be able to access our code. Navigate to the root of our application with package.json and in the console, and use npm install to install the NPM packages we need.

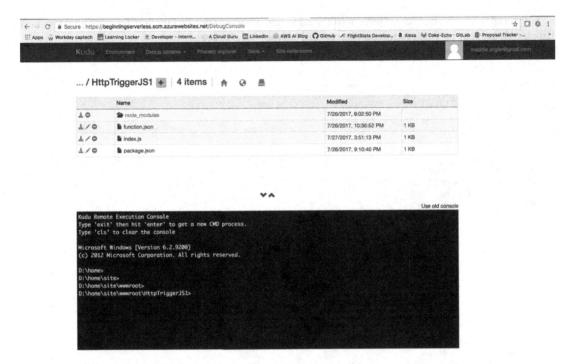

Figure 4-29. This is what the Kudu dashboard looks like when you navigate to the Debug console

---

■ **Note** If the NPM install doesn't work, you can directly drag and drop your `npm_modules` folder into the Kudu project structure. I have had issues in the past with the NPM install from Kudu.

Once your NPM modules are uploaded, we can navigate back to the dashboard and test our function using a POST body that we have used before. Mine looks like this:

```
{
  "name": "Maddie",
  "order": "Mac 'n Cheese",
  "phoneNumber": "1XXXXXXXXXX"
}
```

You use the phone number and order to construct your message. I sent the text to myself to test it out but feel free to pester a friend with your new application. You should receive a text with your message shortly after testing it. To trigger this function outside of the test environment, you can use Postman or another resource and ping the function URL.

To trigger a function, you send an HTTP request to a URL that is a combination of the function app URL and the function name:

```
https://{function app name}.azurewebsites.net/api/{function name}
```

If you specify a method, your URL doesn't need to reference the specific function. So our actual function URL is https://beginningserverless.azurewebsites.net/api/orders/.

And voila! You have a simple customizable notification application (Figure 4-30).

Figure 4-30. *Text from Twilio Messaging Application*

In the next exercise, we will build a storage triggered function that will connect with this application.

ADD TO YOUR FUNCTION

Exercise: Build off this function to add more methods and Azure Functions *proxies*, a preview feature that allows you to forward requests to other resources. You define an HTTP endpoint just like with an HTTP trigger, but instead of writing code to execute when that endpoint is called, you provide a URL to a remote implementation. This allows you to compose multiple API sources into a single API surface that is easy for clients to consume. This is particularly useful if you wish to build your API as microservices. A proxy can point to any HTTP resource, such as these:

- Azure Functions

- API apps

- Docker containers

- Any other hosted API

To learn more, visit `https://docs.microsoft.com/en-us/azure/azure-functions/functions-proxies`.

The Storage Event

For our storage triggered event, we are going to build an application that is triggered by an addition to a queue. To continue with our food theme, we will build an Order queue that will store orders for delivery as they come in. When a new order is added to the queue, we will update our queue and create a POST to our previous function's URL. We are using a queue in this application because it makes sense in the context of delivery. However, there are several storage triggers provided by Azure, including these:

- Azure Blob Storage

- Storage Tables

- SQL Tables

- No-SQL Database

I recommend looking into these other options after our queue demonstration. While the Azure storage options are similar to those in AWS, there are some differences in the way they are set up and accessed. It might be a good idea to read back through Chapter 3 and try to implement our application that we created in AWS in our new Azure environment. That will give you a good benchmark for differences in setup, development, and deployment.

Azure Queue Storage

Azure Queue storage provides cloud messaging between application components. In designing applications for scale, application components are often decoupled, so that they can scale independently. Queue storage delivers asynchronous messaging for communication between application components, whether they are running in the cloud, on the desktop, on an on-premises server, or on a mobile device. Queue storage also supports managing asynchronous tasks and building process work flows.

Figure 4-31 is an example provided by Azure to explain the components of a queue. The example it uses is an image resizing application that is dependent on order. The Queue service contains the following components:

URL Format: Similar to functions, queues are addressable using the following URL format:

`http://<storage account>/queue.core.windows.net/queue`

The following URL addresses the queue in Figure 4-32:

`http://myaccount.queue.core.windows.net/images-to-download`

Storage Account: All access to Azure Storage is done through a storage account.

Queue: A queue contains a set of messages. All messages must be in a queue. Note that the queue name must be all lowercase.

Message: A message, in any format, of up to 64 KB. The maximum time that a message can remain in the queue is 7 days.

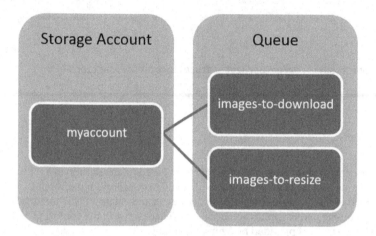

Figure 4-31. *Illustration of the Queue storage that Microsoft Azure provides*

Azure queues are fairly easy to set up and understand so I enjoy working with them. The drawback to queues is the lack of control with the columns and rows. Rows will leave the queue as soon as they are executed (this is how a queue works anyway), and you only have one message column, which is the message being sent. The columns you get from Azure are

- Id

- Insertion Time (UTC)

- Expiration Time (UTC)

- Dequeue count

- Size (bytes)

For the purpose of this exercise, we will be able to accomplish all that we need to do using a queue. However, if you want to add any additional information, you might want to explore using another storage solution.

Create the Function

We are going to return to the Azure portal to create our storage function. To create our Storage function, navigate back to the new functions section and select the QueueTrigger – JavaScript template (Figure 4-32). Leave your storage account connection as is, and change the queue name to whatever makes sense for your queue. I chose orders because my queue is going to be a collection of order.

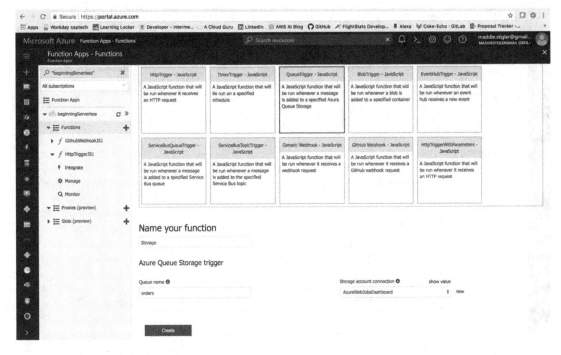

Figure 4-32. *Create a Queue triggered function in Node.js.*

I named my function `Storage` to separate it from the other functions we have already created. Creating this will give you a stubbed-out queue function that you can test using the test box on the right.

You can create a test message and run it to see that it works. However, we haven't set up our queue yet, so we will need to do this. To get started, click on the Documentation tab at the bottom of your integrate blade (Figure 4-33).

■ **Hint** This Documentation tab is actually fairly useful for getting started on any new function. Azure provides its documentation for the functionality of your trigger and function within each function. This makes it really accessible and limits the time you would have spent searching through Stack Overflow and Google.

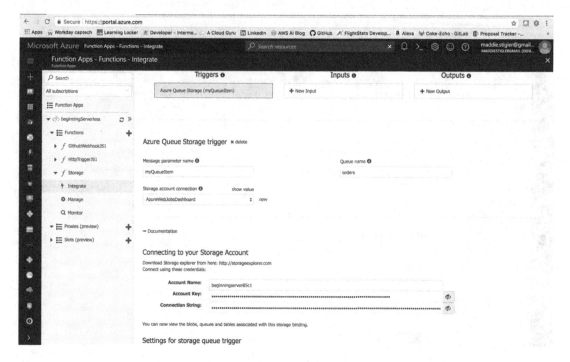

Figure 4-33. *Get the Account Key and the Connection string from your integration documentation*

This Documentation tab contains an Account name, Account Key, and Connections string for your function. You will use the Account name and key to set a connection between the Queue and the function. So copy these values and save them. We are going to create our queue using Microsoft Azure Storage Explorer. You will need to download this tool to be able to use it. We will discuss a little more about Azure Storage Explorer before jumping into it.

Microsoft Azure Storage Explorer

We will be using the Microsoft Azure Storage Explorer tool to access and manipulate our data. Microsoft Azure Storage Explorer (in Preview mode currently) is a standalone app from Microsoft that allows you to work easily with Azure Storage data on Windows, macOS, and Linux. To install this tool, go to `http://storageexplorer.com/` and click the appropriate download package for your machine.

Once Storage Explorer is downloaded, you will need to connect to Azure storage. Click on the third option provided (Use a Storage Account Name and Key) and provide the credentials that we received from the portal earlier. Figure 4-34 shows what your storage attachment should look like.

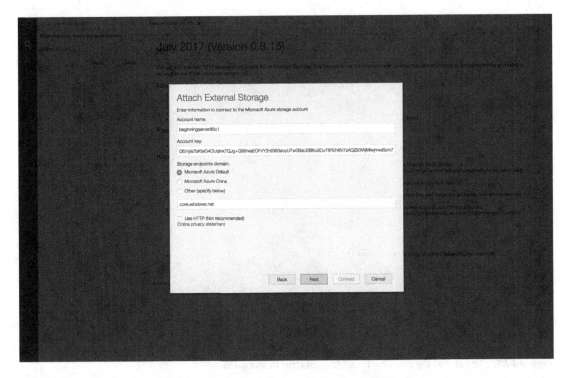

Figure 4-34. *Use the account information to form the connection to our Azure Storage*

Click through the rest of the setup, and this will form the connection to your Azure account and your various Storage capabilities. When the connection is formed, you should see your application listed under Storage Accounts and should see options for Queues, Blob Containers, File Shares, and Tables.

When I first started work, I was assigned an Azure Machine Learning project that used data from a SQL Database. One of my first tasks was to host this data in Azure and I did this through SQL Server. It was an absolute nightmare. This tool is actually very powerful and lets you easily manipulate your data in one spot. The only thing that is a little hard is that it is an entirely new tool you need locally to access these capabilities. I would prefer for this tool to be hosted in Azure but this can be subject to change, seeing as how it is just in Preview mode now. In the meantime, this is what I recommend using when you are interacting with Azure storage.

Under Queues, right-click and choose Create a Queue. Give it the same name you gave it in the settings of your Azure function ("orders"). We can test the template function by clicking Add Message and adding a message to our queue. This should trigger our function; then remove the message from our queue. Figure 4-35 illustrates what our queue should look like.

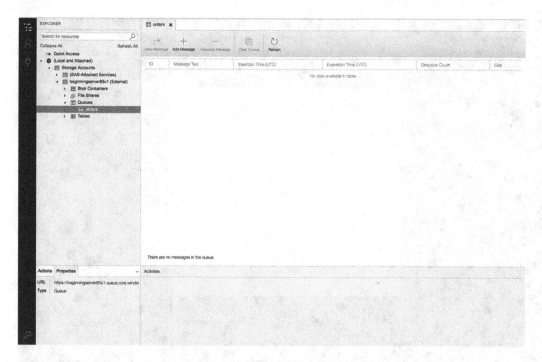

Figure 4-35. *We can test the function by adding an item to our queue*

For my test message, I just provided the queue with a text and sent it on its way (Figure 4-36).

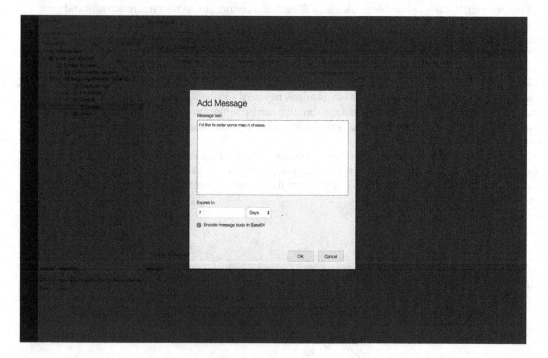

Figure 4-36. *Add a message to your queue*

We can go back to our Azure portal and check the logs for our function to make sure our message was sent and received. If it was successful, you should see a message like the one shown in Figure 4-37.

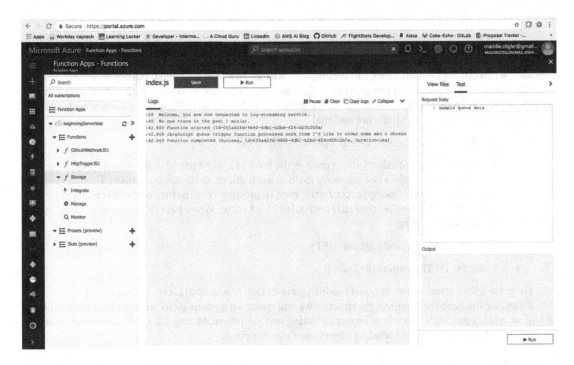

***Figure 4-37.** Success log from our Queue test*

If we have confirmed that our queue is connected to Azure and is triggering our function, we can move on to complete our index, function, and `package.json` files.

Finish Our Function

To write our function, we are going to use our HTTP POST endpoint from the previous exercise to post a request order to it. If you remember, this URL was:

```
https://beginningserverless.azurewebsites.net/api/orders/
```

We will use the Node `request` package to service this request. To do this, we will have to create another `package.json` file and include it in our dependencies. My `package.json` looks like this:

```
{
  "name": "azure-nodejs",
  "version": "1.0.0",
  "description": "Azure Functions for Storage Trigger",
  "main": "handler.js",
  "keywords": [
    "azure",
    "serverless"
  ],
```

```
"dependencies": {
 "request":"^2.81.0"
}
}
```

We need to upload this file to our project in our Azure application. Then we will need to return to our Kudu dashboard and do an NPM install inside our project folder to make sure the right node modules are included to run our application. Once this is complete, we can go ahead and finish out our function.

The Request node module is designed to be the simplest way possible to make http calls. It supports HTTPS and follows redirects by default. The first argument can be either a URL or an options object. The only required option is uri; all others are optional.

- uri || url : Fully qualified URI or a parsed URL object.

- baseUrl: fully qualified uri string used as the base url. Most useful with request. defaults, for example when you want to do many requests to the same domain. If baseUrl is https://example.com/api/, then requesting /end/point?test=true will fetch https://example.com/api/end/point?test=true. When baseUrl is given, uri must also be a string.

- method : HTTP method (default: GET)

- headers : HTTP headers (default: {})

For more information on the Request module, go to https://www.npmjs.com/package/request.

Following the described request parameters, we will create an options JSON with our own values filled in and we will set the JSON variable to be our incoming myQueueItem. Listing 4-2 shows a built-out function for handling Queue requests and sending them to our next function.

Listing 4-2. A function that takes in a queue item and submits it to our HTTP function

```
var request=require('request');

module.exports = function (context, myQueueItem) {
  context.log('JavaScript queue trigger function processed work item', myQueueItem);
  if(myQueueItem.name && myQueueItem.order && myQueueItem.phoneNumber) {

    var options = {
      url: 'https://beginningServerless.azurewebsites.net/api/orders/',
      method: 'POST',
      headers: {
        'Content-Type': 'application/json'
      },
      json: myQueueItem
    };

    request(options, function(err, res, body) {
      if (res && (res.statusCode === 200 || res.statusCode === 201)) {
      console.log(body);
      }
    });
  }
```

```
else (
    console.log("Nothing to process")
)

context.done();
};
```

Once we deploy this function, we can test it by once again creating a message in our queue and submitting it. If all is set up correctly, we should be able to go into our logs for both the Storage function and the HTTP function and see our message come through there. You should also continue receiving texts for each message you create.

■ **Tip** If you are having trouble seeing your changes, make sure your endpoint is correct and that your queue name is the same in Storage Explorer and in Azure. Configuration is more likely your issue than something in your code, and these are the two places where the configuration really matters.

Another thing to keep in mind is that the way we set up our HTTP function was to receive a body in a POST request with a specific structure. The structure was:

```
{
    "name": "",
    "order": "",
    "phoneNumber": "1XXXXXXXXXX"
}
```

So for our HTTP function to be able to handle our incoming queue message properly, one of two things must happen.

1. We must structure all queue messages as if they were JSON objects and make sure each item contains a name, order, and phone number.

2. We must rework our HTTP function to accept a message as a string and send that message directly.

I chose to structure my queue message as a JSON value to test and make sure the message makes it all the way through the flow. After adding the initial message, I first went into my storage function and checked the logs to make sure it received and sent the message. Figure 4-38 shows my results.

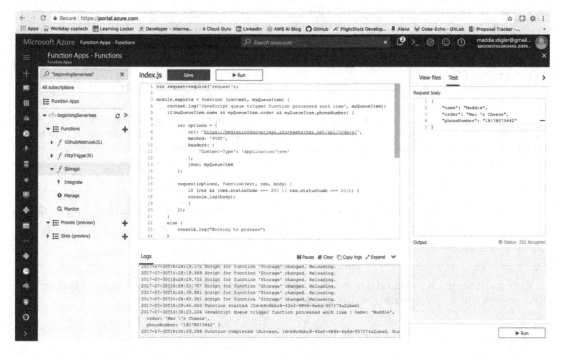

Figure 4-38. *The storage function has been triggered by the message in our queue*

After confirming that the message made it to step one, I looked at our HTTP function logs to make sure it made it through step two as well (Figure 4-39).

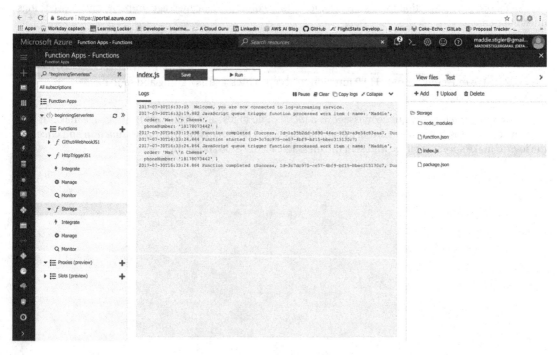

Figure 4-39. *HTTP function logs show the message received and sent via text*

Shortly afterward, I received a text message with the message I had added to the queue. As you can see, it is pretty quick and easy to set up a storage triggered function in Azure, especially using the Storage explorer. The food delivery notification system is one application of the storage as a trigger, but there are many more.

ADD TO YOUR FUNCTION

For this exercise, we are going to restructure our application process flow. The HTTP request will now be step one and the storage event function will be step two. We will continue to use POST requests to our HTTP function, but instead of sending a text, we will update our queue with the parsed message we want to send. When this message is added to the queue, it will trigger the second Lambda function that will send the text to the customer. This will give you exposure to manipulating queue data in Node in Azure functions. If you wanted to take it a step further, you could even look into Blob storage and add images to the storage to send those to the user as well. Azure's blob storage is very similar to AWS S3, which we used in the last chapter. Common uses of Blob storage include these:

- Serving images or documents directly to a browser

- Storing files for distributed access

- Streaming video and audio

- Storing data for backup and restore, disaster recovery, and archiving

- Storing data for analysis by an on-premises or Azure-hosted service

The following diagram should give you a better understanding for how Blob storage works in Azure.

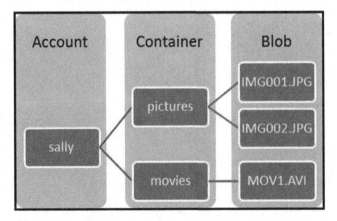

To learn more, visit https://docs.microsoft.com/en-us/azure/storage/storage-nodejs-how-to-use-blob-storage.

Conclusion

In this chapter we explored HTTP triggers and storage triggers in Azure Functions. We looked at some differences between developing in Azure and developing in AWS and discovered a lot of differences in the process of creating functions. We looked into WebHooks and HTTP requests for API triggers and saw how we could use either in daily applications. At this point, you should feel comfortable writing node functions and deploying them in either AWS or Azure. You should have a better understanding of the Azure configurations (and locations of these configurations) in comparison to AWS, and you should have a clearer idea of why you would prefer one vendor over another. In the next chapter, we will continue building Serverless applications. We will look at Google Cloud and build out a couple of Cloud functions, explore the UI, and continue to analyze differences in vendors.

CHAPTER 5

■ ■ ■

Google Cloud

In this chapter, we will use Google Cloud Platform to develop serverless applications and explore differences between Google as a cloud provider and Azure and Amazon as cloud providers. To create these applications, we will use Cloud functions, HTTP requests, Google Cloud Storage bucket, and Cloud Pub/Sub topics. We will also explore different use cases for HTTP and storage triggered functions so we get a better understanding of the breadth and depth of serverless applications. By the end of this chapter, we will have three serverless applications and experience with several Google Cloud services.

■ **Note**   At this book's publication, Google Cloud is currently in a Beta release of Cloud Functions. The APIs might be changed in backward-incompatible ways and are not subject to any SLA or deprecation policies. Keep this in mind while we go through these exercises.

Explore the UI

We are going to start investigating the Google Cloud UI before developing our functions. I would recommend some self-exploration beyond this section to really familiarize yourself with how Google Cloud works. Azure and AWS have many differences, but to me there was definitely more of a learning curve with Google. I think a lot of this had to do with my comfort with AWS and the new concepts introduced in Google Cloud, so we will be sure to explore these differences as we go along. To get started, you will need a Google account to access the Google Cloud UI. After signing into the console at `https://console.cloud.google.com/`, your dashboard will display a list of Google services separated by functionality (very similar to AWS and Azure). Figure 5-1 gives you an idea of all of the services Google Cloud provides.

© Maddie Stigler 2018

M. Stigler, *Beginning Serverless Computing*, https://doi.org/10.1007/978-1-4842-3084-8_5

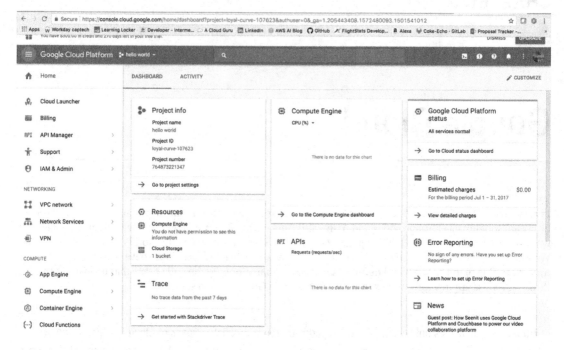

Figure 5-1. *Google Cloud Platform offers many services ranging from compute services to networking services to storage. We will be exploring functions, API manager, storage, and IAM.*

At this point, you have learned a lot of different terms for the same concepts in Amazon and Azure. Table 5-1 provides a concepts map for the three platforms to keep the terminology straight throughout this chapter.

Table 5-1. *Cloud Provider Concepts Table*

Concept	AWS Term	Azure Term	Google Term
Data Center	Region	Region	Region
Abstracted Data Center	Availability Zone	Availability Zones	Zone
Edge Caching	CloudFront		POP (multiple services)
Compute: IaaS	EC2	Virtual Machines	Google Compute Engine
Compute: PaaS	Elastic Beanstalk	App Service, Cloud Services	Google App Engine
Compute: Containers	EC2 Container Service	Azure Container Service, Service Fabric	Google Container Engine
Network: Load Balancing	Elastic Load Balancer	Load Balancer	Load Balancing
Network: Peering	Direct Connect	ExpressRoute	Cloud Interconnect
Network: DNS	Route 53	DNS	Cloud DNS
Storage: Object Storage	S3	Blob	Cloud Storage
Storage: File Storage	Elastic File System	File Storage	Avere

(continued)

Table 5-1. (*continued*)

Concept	AWS Term	Azure Term	Google Term
Database: RDBMS	RDS	SQL Database	Cloud SQL
Database: NoSQL	DynamoDB	Table Storage	Cloud Datastore, Bigtable
Messaging	SNS	Service Bus	Cloud Pub/Sub

Navigation

The dashboard for Google Cloud is pretty straightforward and very accessible. As in Azure, you are able to configure and customize the layout of your dashboard to what works for you. Also similarly to Azure, Google Cloud provides users with a Google Cloud Shell. This can be found in the top right of the blue bar across your dashboard. Google Cloud Shell is an environment for managing resources hosted on Google Cloud Platform.

The shell already has the Cloud SDK up and ready to go. I like this because it's less set up on your local machine and makes it all very accessible through the portal. To test this out, you can open the Cloud Shell and type in:

```
gcloud -version
```

This will give you the list of installed Cloud SDK components and their versions (Figure 5-2).

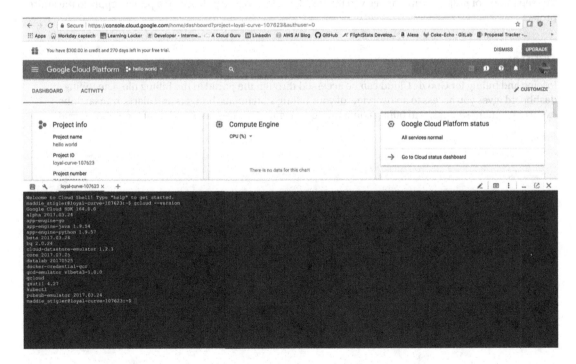

Figure 5-2. *The Cloud Shell comes with Cloud SDK up and running, along with several components*

In the dashboard, we have access to our project info, resources used, billing, and error reporting. The specific project you're in is displayed on the top left of the blue bar. Right now, I am in the Hello World project I created for this tutorial. To create a new project, you can click the drop-down arrow on the blue bar and a project modal will pop up. If you click the plus sign, you can create a new project and add it to your dashboard. Feel free to do this for the Hello World function now.

Any Cloud Platform resources that you allocate and use must belong to a project. I like to think of projects as the organizing entity for what I'm building. A project is made up of the settings, permissions, and other metadata that describe your applications. Resources within a single project can work together easily; for example by communicating through an internal network, subject to the region-and-zone rules. The resources that each project contains remain separate across project boundaries; you can only interconnect them through an external network connection.

By clicking the set of dots next to your profile picture, you have access to a list of other options including Project settings for the given project. When you click this, you see a project ID and a project number. These are the two ways to identify your project. As you work with Cloud Platform, you'll use these identifiers in certain command lines and API calls.

The *project number* is automatically assigned when you create a project.

The *project ID* is a unique identifier for a project. When you first create a project, you can accept the default generated project ID or create your own. A project ID cannot be changed after the project is created, so if you are creating a new project, be sure to choose an ID that will work for the lifetime of the project.

In the same panel, you are able to access IAM permissions and roles for the project. This is a feature that Azure and Google share that AWS does differently. In both Azure and Google, services and resources are split up by project from the console down. In AWS, you can do this but it is not something that is provided out of the box. This means that while navigating through AWS, you would see resources for different projects in the same space and would have to specify IAM policies for specific projects. Google and Azure enforce this separation of projects. Any change you make to Google or Azure policies for a project apply to the entire project.

Pricing

Pricing and billing for Google Cloud can be accessed through the portal in the Billing tile. The Billing dashboard gives you access to an overview of your billing statements, budgets and alerts, transactions, exports, payment settings, and billing configurations. Figure 5-3 gives an overview of the Billing portal.

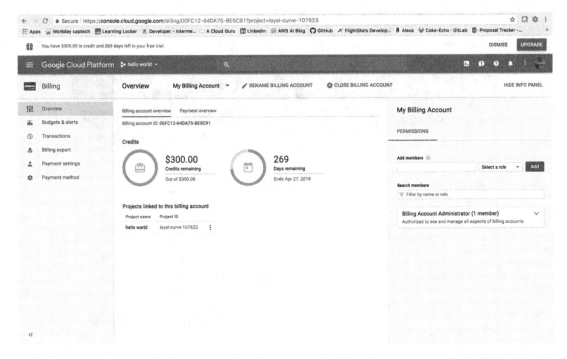

Figure 5-3. *The Billing panel gives you an overview of your billing statements as well as access to permissions to your billing account*

You can create budgets attached to specific projects with a specified amount for various alerts. These alerts will email you when the minimum value submitted has been reached. Google also provides a pricing calculator that is intuitive and easy to use. The other providers we have covered provide this as well.

If you're just working on independent projects, the cost calculator probably matters less to you but if you are ever doing any Cloud architecture and development for someone else, the cost calculator becomes pretty important. Google's calculator lets you pick the services you think you will be using and define all of the specifications for each of them so you will get a more accurate price calculation back. Figure 5-4 shows an estimate for the Hello World cloud function we will be creating together.

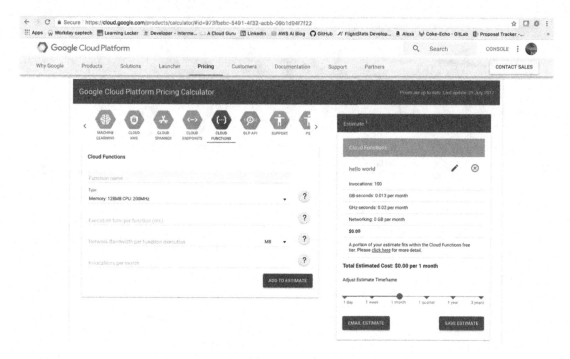

Figure 5-4. *The Cost calculator lets you select the service, information, and add to your current estimate for amount of money per month*

The pricing for Cloud Functions is still incredibly cheap. Cloud Functions are priced according to how long your function runs, how many times it's invoked, and how many resources you provision for the function. If your function makes an outbound network request, there are also additional data transfer fees. Cloud Functions includes a perpetual free tier to allow you to experiment with the platform at no charge.

Cloud Functions

Cloud Functions can be accessed in the left panel under Compute and Functions. Google also gives you a pinning option, so you can keep your access to Functions at the top of your screen no matter where you are in the console. I do this for easy access. The Cloud Functions dashboard lets you view your current active functions, region, trigger, memory allocation per function, and the last deployment. This is also where you would go to create or delete a function. Figure 5-5 gives an overview of the Google Cloud dashboard.

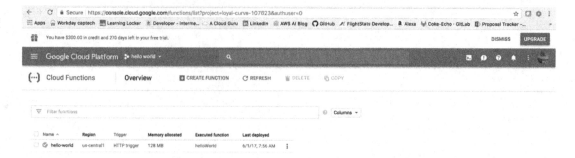

Figure 5-5. *The Cloud functions dashboard shows your active functions and their metrics*

We will walk through creating a function when we begin our Hello World application, but for now, I am going to give a quick background on more specific differences in Google Cloud's functions that Google Cloud specifies in their documentation.

Security IAM

Google Cloud Identity and Access Management (Cloud IAM) enables you to create and manage permissions for Google Cloud Platform resources. Cloud IAM unifies access control for Cloud Platform services into a single system and presents a consistent set of operations.

You can set access control using roles at the project level. Assign a role to a project member or service account to determine the level of access to your Google Cloud Platform project and its resources. By default, all Google Cloud Platform projects come with a single user: the original project creator. No other users have access to the project and or its functions, until a user is added as a project team member. Figure 5-6 demonstrates the IAM flow associated with Google Cloud.

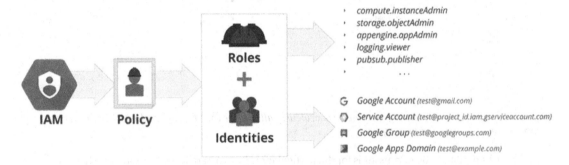

Figure 5-6. *The IAM service attaches a policy to roles and identities to provide secure access*

IAM Console

The IAM console (Figure 5-7) is found under the list of products and services in the left Dashboard blade. The console gives you a dashboard with your current IAM permissions for your project, identity, quotas, service accounts, labels, GCP privacy, settings, encryption keys, proxies, and roles.

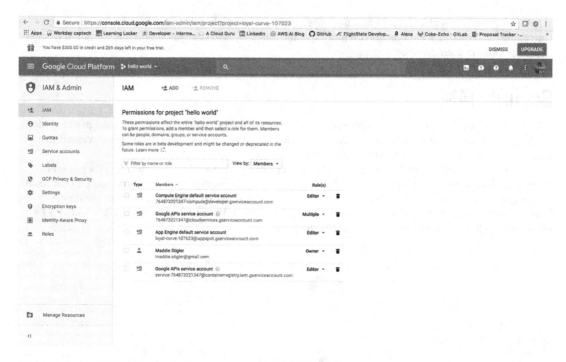

Figure 5-7. *The IAM dashboard gives you an overview of all of your IAM resources along with five security steps you are recommended to complete*

The dashboard lists the permissions for the particular project you are in at the moment. These permissions affect the entire Hello World project and all of its resources. To grant permissions, add a member and then select a role for them. Members can be people, domains, groups, or service accounts.

■ **Note**   At this book's publication, some roles are in Beta development and might be changed or deprecated in the future. These are also basic methodologies that probably won't change. You should be comfortable using roles and services currently in Beta.

Roles

With Cloud IAM, a Cloud API method requires that the identity making the API request has the appropriate permissions to use the resource. You can grant permissions by granting roles to a user, a group, or a service account. There are three types of roles that we will look at: primitive, predefined, and custom roles.

Primitive roles are roles that existed prior to Cloud IAM. Owner, Editor, and Viewer will continue to work as they did before. These roles are concentric; that is, the Owner role includes the permissions in the Editor role, and the Editor role includes the permissions in the Viewer role. Primitive roles can be assigned at the project level.

Cloud IAM provides additional *predefined roles* that give granular access to specific Google Cloud Platform resources and prevent unwanted access to other resources. You can grant multiple roles to the same user. For example, the same user can have Network Admin and Log Viewer roles on a project and also have a Publisher role for a Pub/Sub topic within that project.

In addition to predefined roles, Cloud IAM also provides the ability to create *customized roles.* You can create a custom IAM role with one or more permissions and then grant that custom role to users who are part of your organization (Figure 5-8).

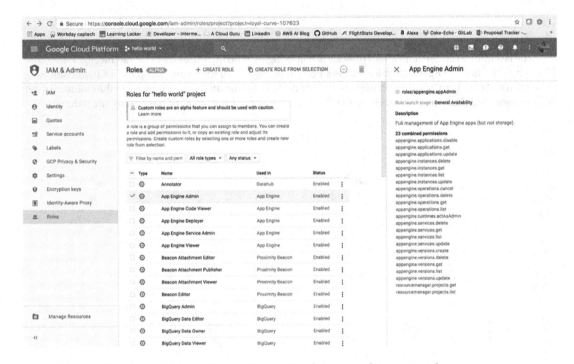

Figure 5-8. *The list of available roles through Google Cloud. You can also create a role.*

Policies

You can grant roles to users by creating a *Cloud IAM policy*, which is a collection of statements that define who has what type of access. A policy is attached to a resource and is used to enforce access control whenever that resource is accessed.

A Cloud IAM policy is represented by the policy object. A *policy* consists of a list of bindings. A *binding* binds a list of members to a role. The following code snippet shows the structure of a Cloud IAM policy:

```
{
 "bindings": [
  {
   "role": "roles/owner",
   "members": [
    "user:maddie@example.com",
    "group:admins@example.com",
    "domain:google.com",
    "serviceAccount:my-other-app@appspot.gserviceaccount.com",
   ]
  },
```

```
  {
    "role": "roles/viewer",
    "members": ["user:maddie@example.com"]
  }
 ]
}
```

The last thing to understand about policies is that Google Cloud organizes them hierarchically. This hierarchy is defined by Organization ä Projects ä Resources. Figure 5-9 shows an example of a Cloud Platform resource hierarchy. The Organization node is the root node in the hierarchy, the Projects are the children of the Organization, and the other Resources are the children of Projects. Each resource has exactly one parent.

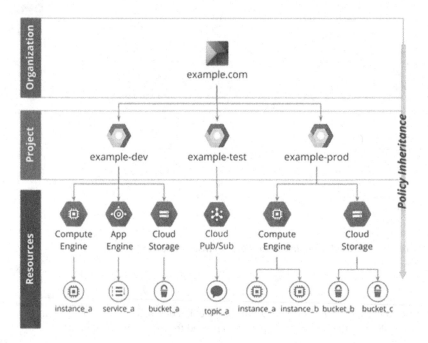

Figure 5-9. *The list of roles available through Google Cloud. You can also create a role.*

Your First Code

Now that we have a better understanding of Google Cloud and its capabilities, we can begin creating our serverless applications using Google Functions. If you already have the project, SDK, Billing, and API set up, you can proceed to the Hello World section. If not, please take the five minutes to set these things up.

To set up the project, go to the Projects page: `https://console.cloud.google.com/project`. Create a new Hello World project in this space. We will also need to enable billing. Take the following steps to do this:

1. From the projects list, select the project to re-enable billing for.

2. Open the console left side menu and select Billing.

3. Click Link a Billing Account.

4. Click Set Account.

Next, we want to enable the Cloud Functions API:

1. From the projects list, select a project or create a new one.

2. If the API Manager page isn't already open, open the console left side menu and select API Manager, and then select Library.

3. Click the Cloud Functions API.

4. Click ENABLE.

You can install the Google Cloud SDK by downloading the correct package from here:

`https://cloud.google.com/sdk/docs/`

At this point, you should have all of the prerequisites in place to begin developing our serverless functions.

Hello World

We will start by creating a new function in the Cloud Functions console. To get here, navigate to Cloud Functions from the dashboard. As shown in Figure 5-10, we will create a new function, name it `hello-world`, and give it the following properties:

- **Name:** hello-world
- **Region:** us-central1
- **Memory Allocated:** 128 MB
- **Timeout:** 60 seconds
- **Trigger:** HTTP trigger
- **Bucket:** hello-world

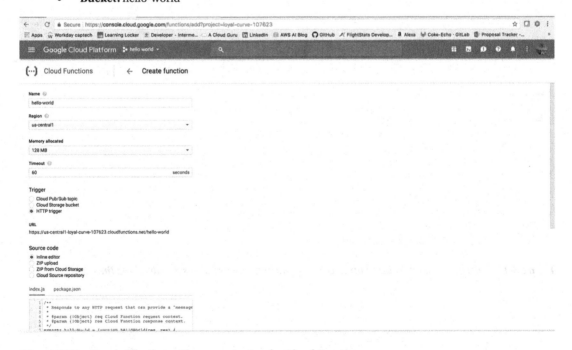

Figure 5-10. *Google Cloud provides an easy setup for Cloud Functions*

We are going to select an HTTP trigger to make this a base function for our HTTP trigger function. Google is similar to Azure in that it provides you with a URL to access and trigger your HTTP functions. With this, we can test and run our function without having to stand up an entire API. Configuration for any function requires a name, trigger, region, memory, timeout, source code and source bucket. Names do not have to be unique universally, just within your functions. Google Cloud also gives you the choice of editing your code inline or uploading a zip. Since this function is going to be simple and small, we can edit it inline.

The hello-world HTTP triggered function Google provides you with simply takes the incoming request body and returns it to the console for the user to see. The function responds to any HTTP request that can provide a "message" field in the body. To test it and get comfortable with the new environment, we will stick with the hello-world HTTP function provided by Google. Once it is created, you should see it pop up in the list of functions. If you click on the function, you will have access to general monitoring, trigger configuration, source code, and testing.

If we look at testing, there is an input box that lets us define the triggering event. There is also an output box that will show us the results from the logs. To start, let's create a test event that just says Hi to us.

```
{
"message": "Hi Maddie"
}
```

Figure 5-11 shows this test method in execution.

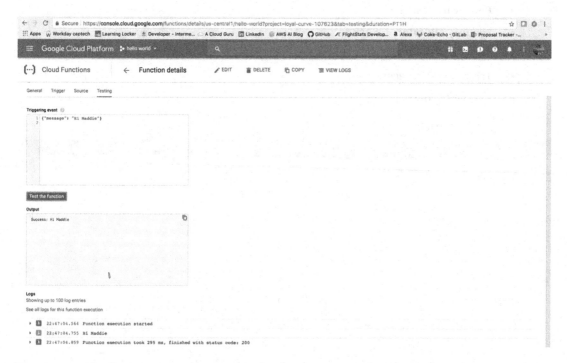

Figure 5-11. *This function returns an output equal to the input and sends us logs detailing the trigger*

The function should trigger an output very similar to the input and should also trigger logging for the function. If you click "See all logs for this function execution," you will be taken to Stackdriver logging. You should also be able to access this publicly. If you grab the URL for the function and copy it into Postman with a request, you should get the same result (Figure 5-12).

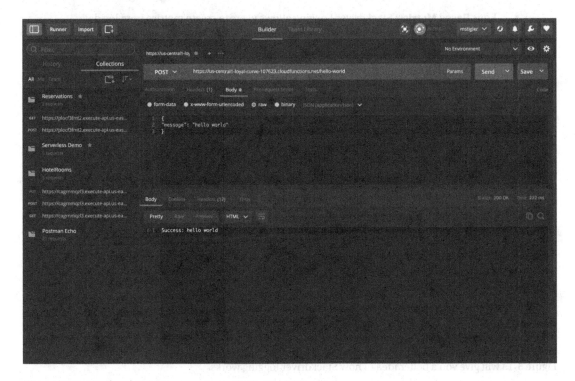

Figure 5-12. *Postman POST request to our Hello World function*

Next, we are going to look at Stackdriver logging. This is helpful for debugging and for the construction of our function.

Stackdriver Logging

Stackdriver logging allows us to store, search, analyze, monitor, and alert on log data and events from Google Cloud Platform and AWS. I actually haven't used this with AWS yet, but the integration is an important step. A lot of companies fear transition to the cloud due to vendor lock-in. Providers that embrace this fear and provide solutions for it are making the right move by being more integrative.

The Stackdriver API takes in any log data from any source. This is great because it also allows analysis of this log data in real time. Stackdriver logging includes these features:

- **Custom Logs / Ingestion API:** Stackdriver Logging has a public API which can be used to write any custom log, from any source, into the service.

- **AWS Integration / Agent:** Stackdriver Logging uses a Google-customized and packaged Fluentd agent that can be installed on any AWS or Cloud Platform VMs to ingest log data from Cloud Platform instances (Compute Engine, Managed VMs, Containers) as well as AWS EC2 instances.

- **Logs Retention:** Allows you to retain the logs in Stackdriver Logging for 30 days, and gives you a one-click configuration tool to archive data for a longer period in Google Cloud Storage.

- **Logs Search:** A powerful interface to search, slice and dice, and browse log data.

- **Logs Based Metrics:** Stackdriver Logging allows users to create metrics from log data which appear seamlessly in Stackdriver Monitoring, where users can visualize these metrics and create dashboards.

- **Logs Alerting:** Integration with Stackdriver Monitoring allows you to set alerts on the logs events, including the log-based metrics you have defined.

- **Advanced Analytics with BigQuery:** Take out data with one-click configuration in real time to BigQuery for advanced analytics and SQL-like querying.

- **Archive with Cloud Storage:** Export log data to Google Cloud Storage to archival so you can store data for longer periods of time in a cost effective manner.

- **Stream Logs with Cloud Pub/Sub:** Stream your logging data via Cloud Pub/Sub with a third party solution or a custom endpoint of your choice.

- Splunk & Logentries Integration - Stackdriver Logging supports easy integration with Splunk and Logentries (Rapid7).

- Audit Logging - Stackdriver Logs Viewer, APIs, and the gCloud CLI can be used to access Audit Logs that capture all the admin and data access events within the Google Cloud Platform.

Stackdriver reminds me a lot of CloudWatch in AWS. AWS provides options to send CloudWatch logs into Elasticsearch. This gives you a lot of the same features we are looking at in Google Cloud Stackdriver. It is a central repository for all logging. If you navigate to it after triggering our hello world project, you will see all of the logs for that action. They are sorted by time period and give you the exact request that comes in. Figure 5-13 will give you a better idea of how Stackdriver logging works.

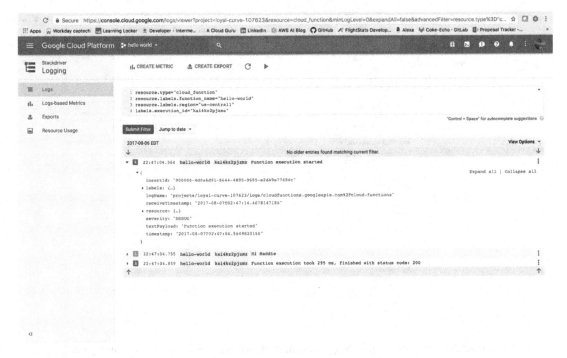

Figure 5-13. *Stackdriver gives you access to metrics, exports of logging, and logging on a function for a particular date*

Stackdriver gives you access to logs, metrics, traces, and other signals from your infrastructure platform(s), virtual machines, containers, middleware, and application tier, so that you can track issues all the way from your end user to your backend services and infrastructure. Native support for distributed systems, auto-scaling, and ephemeral resources means that your monitoring works seamlessly with your modern architecture.

If you click on the Google Cloud hamburger icon, you will see an entire section devoted to Stackdriver. This section includes Monitoring, Debugging, Logging, Trace, and error reporting. We will mostly be using logging, but it is good to learn about the complete functionality of Stackdriver.

Stackdriver Debugger (Figure 5-14) lets you inspect the state of an application at any code location without stopping or slowing it down. The debugger makes it easier to view the application state without adding logging statements. To give an example of how we could use the debugger, I'm going to go to the console and enable the debugger to access my GitHub.

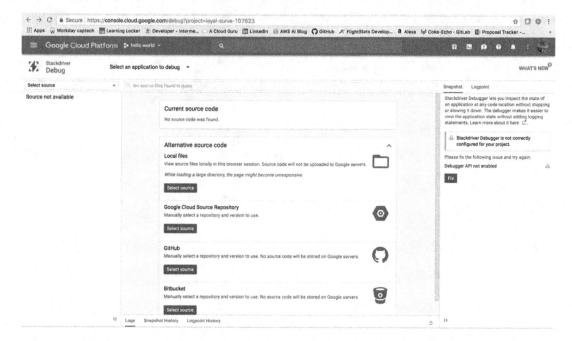

Figure 5-14. *Stackdriver allows you to debug your code and provides several options for source code*

GitHub will ask you to grant Google Cloud access to your repo. When you do this, you can select a source from your repo that you want to look at. I have been working on an Alexa Skills project with some co-workers, so I am going to open that repo up and take a look. Feel free to explore some of your own code. Your users are not impacted during debugging. Using the production debugger (Figure 5-15) you can capture the local variables and call stack and link it back to a specific line location in your source code. You can use this to analyze the production state of your application and understand the behavior of your code in production.

Figure 5-15. *Stackdriver lets you look at production code in debugging mode*

Stage Bucket

Google Cloud uses the idea of a stage *bucket* to stage and deploy your code in Google Cloud. We will look more into buckets during the creation of our Storage Trigger function, but it will be useful to see a high-level overview now. In Google, the Buckets resource represents a bucket in Google Cloud Storage. There is one global namespace shared by all buckets. This means every bucket name must be unique.

Buckets (Figure 5-16) contain objects, which can be accessed by their own methods. In addition to the ACL property, buckets contain bucketAccessControls, for use in fine-grained manipulation of an existing bucket's access controls. A bucket is always owned by the project team owners group.

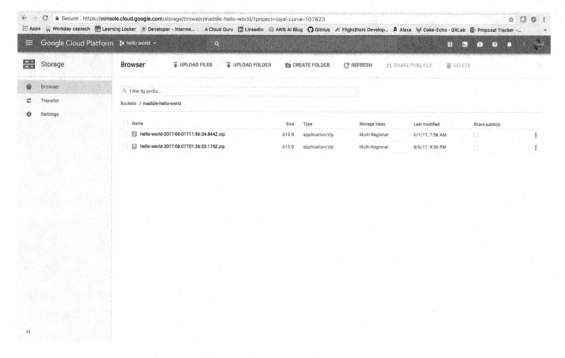

Figure 5-16. *The storage bucket for my Cloud Function*

This is where our Cloud function code is being stored. You can access it from the bucket. You can also create, upload files, and upload folders. This interface is very similar to AWS S3 to me. It is very simple to use, easy to understand, and easy to access.

Before continuing to our HTTP event triggered function, we are going to add a couple things to our Hello World function. Request parameters that we should learn include:

- Request.method (for example, POST)

- Request.get('x-myheader') (for example, "123")

- Request.query.foo (for example, "baz")

- Request.body.text (for example, "something")

We are going to elaborate on our Hello World function so it is able to handle different types of requests. We will use the request.method parameter to specify which action to take in which case. The code in Listing 5-1 demonstrates how to handle this.

Listing 5-1. This code shows how to handle multiple HTTP requests within one file.

```
function handlePUT(req, res) {
 //handle put request
 console.log(req.body.message);
 res.status(200).send('PUT Success: ' + `Hello ${name || 'World'}!`);
};
```

```
function handleGET(req, res) {
 //handle get request
 }
 console.log(req.body.message);
 res.status(200).send('GET Success: ' + `Hello ${name || 'World'}!`);
};

/**
 * @param {Object} req Cloud Function request context.
 * @param {Object} res Cloud Function response context.
 */
exports.helloWorld = function helloWorld (req, res) {
 let name =null;
 switch (req.method) {
  case 'GET':
   handleGET(req, res);
   break;
  case 'PUT':
   handlePUT(req, res);
   break;
  default:
   res.status(500).send({ error: 'Something blew up!' });
   break;
 }
};
```

In this code, we are changing our response based on the request type. You should be able to see these results in Postman. You can see how we'll be able to use this to our advantage later on. Within serverless architecture, it is usually better practice to separate these requests from each other in the code. For this, you would have a Cloud function for each request that handles one execution.

We can still use the request.method property here in our more singular functions to double check that the requests coming in are valid. It is also important to know the structure of the requests coming in. The body of the request is automatically parsed based on the content type and populated in the body of the request object. Figure 5-17 demonstrates the request types that Google accepts.

Content Type	Request Body	Behavior
application/json	'{"name":"John"}'	request.body.name equals 'John'
application/octet-stream	'my text'	request.body equals '6d792074657874' (see Node.js Buffer docs)
text/plain	'my text'	request.body equals 'my text'
application/x-www-form-urlencoded	'name=John'	request.body.name equals 'John'

Figure 5-17. *Example request bodies for various content types*

We can test the different request bodies using switch statements similar to the ones we wrote to determine the method. Inside our POST and GET functions, we will include a switch statement that looks for the content type and returns the appropriate response. The following code demonstrates this.

```
/**
 * @param {Object} req Cloud Function request context.
 * @param {Object} res Cloud Function response context.
 */
exports.helloWorld = function helloWorld (req, res) {
 let name =null;
 switch (req.method) {
  case 'GET':
   handleGET(req, res);
   break;
  case 'PUT':
   handlePUT(req, res);
   break;
  default:
   res.status(500).send({ error: 'Something blew up!' });
   break;
 }
};

function handlePUT(req, res) {
 //handle put request
  switch (req.get('content-type')) {
  // '{"name":"Maddie"}'
  case 'application/json':
   name = req.body.name;
   break;

  // 'name=Maddie'
  case 'application/x-www-form-urlencoded':
   name = req.body.name;
   break;
 }
 console.log(req.body.message);
 res.status(200).send('PUT Success: ' + `Hello ${name || 'World'}!`);
};

function handleGET(req, res) {
 //handle get request
  switch (req.get('content-type')) {
  // '{"name":"Maddie"}'
  case 'application/json':
   name = req.body.name;
   break;
```

```
  // 'name=Maddie'
  case 'application/x-www-form-urlencoded':
    name = req.body.name;
    break;
  }
  console.log(req.body.message);
  res.status(200).send('GET Success: ' + `Hello ${name || 'World'}!`);
};
```

If we test this in Postman using a PUT request with a JSON object, we should receive the response defined in the handle PUT under the application/json content type (Figure 5-18).

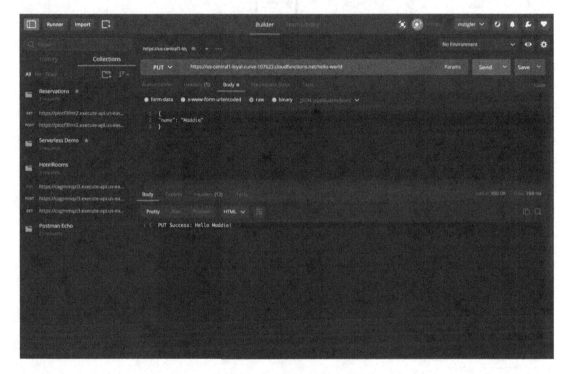

Figure 5-18. *The Postman PUT request returns the response specified under the PUT function with the application/JSON switch case statement*

Now that we have a basic understanding of handling requests and responses in Google Cloud functions, we can move on to creating a more full-fledged HTTP trigger function.

HTTP Event

Our HTTP triggered function is going to utilize several components of Google Cloud to create a notification system. For the HTTP event, we will utilize a POST request and Firebase Realtime database. I am currently working on an Alexa Skills project that creates requests for guests from their hotel room. I'm going to base the functionality of this function on that system.

Our application is going to take an incoming POST request with a room number and service request and post it to a database. Our HTTP event will handle POST requests with new guest information and will add the information to a guest storage bucket. The storage function will then be triggered by this object upload and will integrate with Firebase to notify the guest. Figure 5-19 shows the plan for the overall architecture of the next couple of exercises.

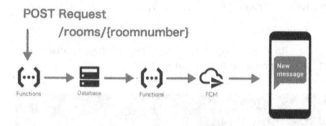

Figure 5-19. *The POST request will take a room number and add guest data to it in the database*

To start, we will go ahead and create another HTTP trigger function. I chose to create a new storage bucket just to keep all function services together. I also changed the function to execute to `httpTrigger` and changed this in the sample code as well. Figure 5-20 shows what my new function's configuration should look like.

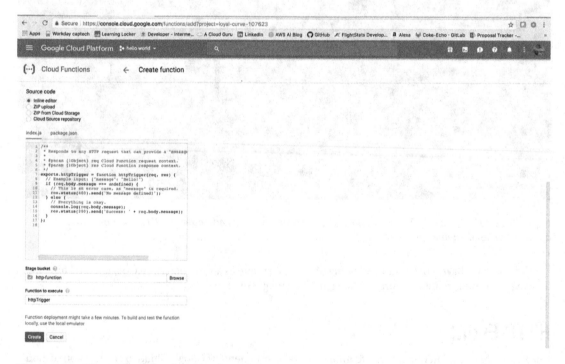

Figure 5-20. *The configuration for* `http-function`

Before we continue developing this skeleton of a function, we are going to set up our Firebase environment. In this aspect of the project, we will use Firebase to create a database and integrate it with our Cloud function. To connect a function to Firebase Hosting, we will need to set up Cloud Functions, write our function, create rewrite rules, and deploy our changes.

Firebase Realtime Database

The Firebase Realtime Database is a cloud-hosted database. Data is stored as JSON and synchronized in Realtime to every connected client. This is perfect for our use case because we can just store JSON objects of guests and room numbers. When you build cross-platform apps with our iOS, Android, and JavaScript SDKs, all of your clients share one Realtime Database instance and automatically receive updates with the newest data. Some applications of Google Firebase include:

- **Serving dynamic content:** You can perform server-side logic through a function to return a dynamically generated response.

- **Pre-rendering for SPA to improve SEO:** This allows us to create dynamic meta tags for sharing across various social networks.

- **Lightweight Web App:** We can create an API with our Cloud functions for our Firebase hosting site to asynchronously retrieve content.

One of the more confusing aspects of Firebase and Google Cloud to me was the difference between the two. They are pretty integrated with one another and share a lot of the same resources and functionality. You will notice this as you navigate the Firebase portal. While Firebase is primarily for mobile apps, you can use the scalable and infrastructure-free aspects of it to quickly set up and deploy serverless applications. You can later integrate these applications with mobile platforms, or continue running them as is.

When you first start with Firebase, you will be prompted to create a project or to import one from Google Cloud. For our application, we are going to build within Firebase to get exposure to this environment. However, what I recommend doing after this exercise is to build all of your functions within a project in Google Cloud and import the entire project into Firebase.

To create an application that utilizes Firebase, we must follow a couple of steps to prep our function. First make sure you have the latest version of the Firebase CLI. You can install the latest version of the Firebase CLI by running the following command in your terminal:

```
npm install -g firebase-tools
```

This will install the Firebase toolkit on your terminal. We are going to use this to access a Firebase project and deploy it using Cloud functions. It has a similar functionality to the serverless framework in this regard. We will be able to completely deploy our project using Firebase tools instead of having to zip and upload a project folder. Once you install Firebase tools using NPM, your terminal should look something like Figure 5-21 if Firebase installs successfully.

Figure 5-21. *Firebase will install and give you different project deployment options*

Firebase provides you with a URL to log in to your Google Cloud account. This will allow you to deploy to your cloud environment directly. Once you are authorized, you can begin initializing Firebase projects in the current directory. However, before doing this, you will need to return to the Firebase console and create an existing project with Hosting. To do this, navigate to console.firebase.google.com and click Create a New Project. I named mine http-project (Figure 5-22).

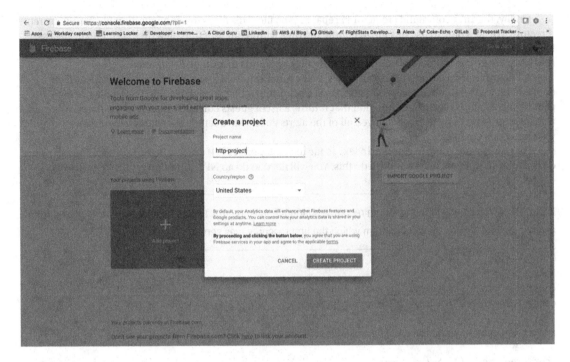

Figure 5-22. Create a new project in Firebase to connect our function to Firebase hosting

After creating a project, we can initialize it back in our terminal with the command:

```
firebase use -add
```

This will prompt you to select your project and create an alias for it. Go ahead and select the project you created. I chose staging as my alias, but feel free to name yours as you please. After this, we have an existing project with hosting and can run the following command within our project directory to initialize cloud functions:

```
firebase init functions
```

This command does a couple of things. First, it creates a functions directory with an index.js file. This is your cloud function file that we will be editing. Second, the command adds a .firebaserc file to your project directory. This file is where your alias definitions are written. We don't need to change this, but feel free to take a look and see how the alias is defined. Mine looks like the following:

```
{
 "projects": {
  "staging": "http-project-6da2a",
  "default": "http-project-6da2a"
 }
}
```

Finally, the `init` command creates a `firebase.json` file. This file is the configuration file for our current directory. We are going to use this file to handle rewrites within our function. Rewrites aren't really necessary for our application, but we will go through an example of using them just to be comfortable with them. With rewrite rules, we can direct requests that match specific patterns to a single destination.

An example of this would be executing a specific function when a particular page is reached. In our application, we can think of several situations where this might be handy. We could have a rewrite for a `/guests` page that triggers a guest function that returns a list of guests currently staying at the hotel. We could also have an `/alerts` page that displayed all of the alerts guests have sent in. Keep these in mind as you build your functions out later.

For now, we are going to edit our `index.js` file to display our HTTP request in the browser. The following code shows an example of how we will do this. You will need to do an NPM install to get the `cors` module.

■ **Note**   CORS stands for cross-origin resource sharing. Enabling `cors` allows resources to be accessed from another domain outside the domain from which the first resource was served.

```
'use strict';
const functions = require('firebase-functions');
const cors = require('cors')({origin: true});

exports.alerts = functions.https.onRequest((req, res) => {

  cors(req, res, () => {
   let request = req.query.alert;
   let roomnumber = req.query.roomNumber;
   console.log("alert " + alert + " room " + roomnumber);
   if (!request) {
    request = req.body.alert;
    roomnumber = req.body.roomNumber;
 }
   res.status(200).send(`<!doctype html>
   <head>
    <title>Incoming Request</title>
   </head>
   <body>
    Request: ${alert}
    </br>
    RoomNumber: ${roomnumber}
   </body>
  </html>`);
  });
});
```

The code takes the incoming request and separates it based on its query. It then returns the request to the user in HTML format. We will also want to edit our `firebase.json` file to redirect our request based on the method. The following code is how I chose to redirect my function:

```
{
 "hosting": {
  "public": "functions",
  "rewrites": [
   {
    "source": "/alerts",
    "function": "alerts"
   }
  ]
 }
}
```

This specifies the folder that our project is pulling from, the source we want our requests to be directed to, and the name of the function we want to execute. To deploy this function, we will use the `firebase deploy` command in our root directory:

```
firebase deploy
```

Figure 5-23 shows the result.

Figure 5-23. *The deployment of our* `index.js` *file to our Firebase hosting environment*

Once your code has successfully deployed, we can test the functionality by simply hitting the function's URL in our browser. To do this, enter the following URL with your request:

```
https://us-central1-<project name>.cloudfunctions.net/alerts?alert=<your
alert>&roomnumber=<number>
```

This will submit the request to your function that you created and return the response you specified (Figure 5-24).

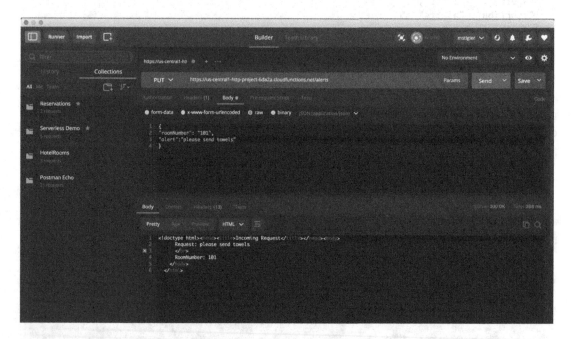

Figure 5-24. *The request is formatted and displayed in your browser*

Obviously, this isn't the most glamorous way to display our information in the browser, but it still gives you a feel for how Cloud Functions integrates with Firebase and the different applications to this integration. You can also access this request in Postman (Figure 5-25). You can take the query strings and make them a part of the body of the request to test the different ways to access our information.

Figure 5-25. *Postman accepts the same request and will accept a JSON body format*

In this exercise, we have used Cloud Functions with Firebase to develop an application that takes an incoming POST request, presents it in the browser, and submits it to a Firebase Realtime database. Now that we know our function is being triggered, let's do something real with the information coming in. We are going to build off our current serverless function to allow the data coming in to be stored in a Firebase Realtime database. To do this, we are going to edit our function to connect to a database that we name and push each incoming entry into the database. The following code demonstrates this concept in action.

```
'use strict';
const functions = require('firebase-functions');
const admin = require('firebase-admin');
admin.initializeApp(functions.config().firebase);
const cors = require('cors')({origin: true});
const storageModule = require('./storage');
```

```
exports.alerts = functions.https.onRequest((req, res) => {

 cors(req, res, () => {
  let alert = req.query.alert;
  let roomnumber = req.query.roomNumber;
  let phoneNumber = req.query.phoneNumber;
  let name = req.query.name;
  console.log("alert " + alert + " room " + roomnumber);
  if (!alert) {
   alert = req.body.alert;
   roomnumber = req.body.roomNumber;
   phoneNumber = req.body.phoneNumber;
   name = req.body.name;
  }
  admin.database().ref('/alerts').push({alert: alert, roomnumber:roomnumber, phoneNumber:
  phoneNumber, name: name}).then(snapshot => {
  });
  res.status(200).send(`<!doctype html>
  <head>
   <title>Incoming Request</title>
  </head>
  <body>
   Request: ${alert}
   </br>
   RoomNumber: ${roomnumber}
  </body>
 </html>`);
 });
});

exports.sendAlert = functions.database.ref('/alerts/{pushId}').onWrite(storageModule.
handler);
```

The Realtime database is a NoSQL database and as such has different optimizations and functionality than a relational database. The Realtime Database API is designed to allow only operations that can be executed quickly. This enables us to build a great real-time experience that can serve millions of users without compromising on responsiveness.

As you can see in this code, we are first checking the incoming request parameters to see if the request is coming in through the query string or a JSON body. We then parse the request and feed it to the Alerts path in the Realtime database for our project.

Once you have this code fleshed out, we can go ahead and redeploy it to our application. We will use the same `firebase deploy` command.

■ **Note**   We are using the `cors` module in this exercise, so make sure you have added it to your `package.json` file and have installed it in the root folder with the `npm install` command before deploying.

When the code is deployed, we can test our changes by hitting the same URL in the browser. We will use the same alert and roomNumber query strings to ping the function. We can check the success of our function in a couple of ways.

If we navigate back to the Firebase portal, on the left side you will see a Database option. Clicking this will take you to the Database console with the real-time data. You should see a structured data table under the name of your project. Below the project name, you will see any paths you have created and the data associated with each. My Database panel looks like Figure 5-26.

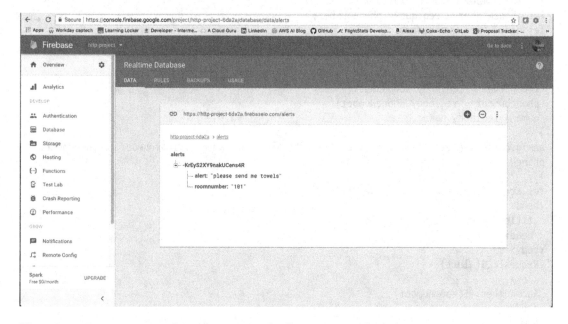

Figure 5-26. *Postman accepts the same request and will accept a JSON body format*

The `alert` and `roomnumber` are associated with a particular key that is generated upon the request. You can add as many properties as you would like and they would change dynamically with the request. The Firebase Realtime database data is stored as JSON objects. Google likes to describe the structure as a cloud-hosted JSON tree. Unlike SQL, there are no tables or records. All data added simply becomes a new node in the existing JSON structure with an associated key.

You do have the ability to provide your own keys in your POST request. Google also recommends several best practices for structuring your data, which we'll look at next.

■ **Tip** For NoSQL beginners, feel free to explore this site to learn your way around this concept: `https://www.w3schools.com/nodejs/nodejs_mongodb.asp`

Avoid Nesting Data

Because the Firebase Realtime Database allows nesting data up to 32 levels deep, you might be tempted to think that this should be the default structure. However, when you fetch data at a location in your database, you also retrieve all of its child nodes. In addition, when you grant someone read or write access at a node in your database, you also grant them access to all data under that node. Therefore, in practice, it's best to keep your data structure as flat as possible.

Flatten Data Structures

If the data is instead split into separate paths, also called denormalization, it can be efficiently downloaded in separate calls, as it is needed.

Create Data That Scales

When building apps, it's often better to download a subset of a list. This is particularly common if the list contains thousands of records. When this relationship is static and one-directional, you can simply nest the child objects under the parent.

Sometimes, this relationship is more dynamic, or it may be necessary to denormalize this data. Many times you can denormalize data by using a query to retrieve a subset of the data. However, even this may be insufficient. Consider, for example, a two-way relationship between users and groups. Users can belong to a group, and a group comprises a list of users. When it comes time to decide which groups a user belongs to, things get complicated.

IMPROVING OUR SERVERLESS FUNCTION

Improve by enforcing strongly typed variables and authorization

Create strongly typed variables:

1. Use TypeScript and create models for our incoming requests. This will enforce structure in both our code and our requests. Example:

```
export interface alertModel {
    alert: string,
    roomNumber: string
}
```

2. Require that incoming requests meet this model to make sure we aren't getting random data in our requests or invalid data in our requests.

3. Check the request method before handling the request. We want to look only at POST and PUT requests in this case. GET requests would be handled differently. Utilize the switch statements we created in Hello World to implement this.

Add an authorization piece:

1. Currently, our function is wide open to any and all requests coming through our HTTP endpoint. With a production application we would not want that to be the case. There are a couple of ways to handle this, one of them being creating an authorization header.

---

2. Use the Firebase Id token along with the request in the Authorization header to verify the request using the Firebase Admin SDK. There is a good example of this implementation on GitHub at

    `https://github.com/firebase/functions-samples/blob/master/`
    `authorized-https-endpoint/functions/index.js`

The code for both of these improvements on the project can be found here: `https://github.com/`
`mgstigler/Serverless/tree/master/AWS/aws-service/HTTPTrigger`

In the next section, we will use the skills and tools we learned with the HTTP Trigger to create a separate Google Cloud function triggered by a storage event in Firebase.

Storage Event

In this section we will continue developing our notification application for hotel guests by incorporating a storage trigger event that sends our storage function into action. We will use the data POST from the previous exercise as this storage trigger. Once our function is triggered, we will use Twilio again to send off a message to the customer.

Before we get going, we will need to make a couple of changes to our current HTTP function. We want to be able to store the guest's name and phone number in addition to their request and room number. To do this, go back to your function and make sure these fields are of types that can be submitted either by query string or by JSON post body. Once that is done, we can begin creating our function.

Create our Storage Triggered Function

As I mentioned earlier, we are deploying this application through Firebase to learn something new and to demonstrate different approaches. Unfortunately, we are about to experience one of the pain points of this deployment method and that is multiple functions per project.

To be able to handle this change, we are going to restructure our project code a bit. Figure 5-27 shows the `functions` folder with our index JavaScript file and an additional `storage.js` file. We are going to place our second function directly in this folder and will handle separate requests within the `index.js` file.

Figure 5-27. *We are going to create another JavaScript file within our current project structure to demonstrate how Firebase splits up functions in its environment*

The reason we need to include this file directly in our functions folder within our HTTP trigger event is because we need access to the HTTP event Realtime database. We do not have access to databases between projects, so we will deploy the two functions together.

Later, we will see an example of how we can deploy all of our functions through the Google Cloud environment and still have them show up in Firebase as separate entities. To be able to reference the code that we will be using in the storage.js file, we will need to include it in the index.js file.

The following code demonstrates how I have implemented this.

```
'use strict'
const functions = require('firebase-functions');
const admin = require('firebase-admin');

admin.initializeApp(functions.config().firebase);
const cors = require('cors')({ origin : true });
const storageModule = require('./storage');
```

We first require the `storage.js` file to be used in our index file.

```
exports.sendAlert =
functions.database.ref('/alerts/{pushId}').onWrite(storageModule.handler);
```

Then we can use this variable to call the handler in our `storage.js` file whenever a new item is written to our Realtime database. You can test this by just putting a `console.log` in your storage file and seeing if it is triggered when the index file is triggered.

We will go ahead and deploy this function to make sure Firebase is recognizing two separate Cloud functions. Within the Firebase console, we can navigate to Functions and see the active functions (Figure 5-28). If it deployed correctly, you will see two separate functions: `alerts` and `sendAlert`. You will also notice the different trigger events for each. You should see a `Write` event for the `sendAlert` function.

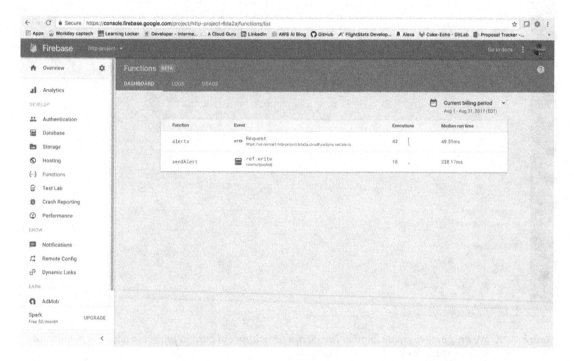

Figure 5-28. *Firebase separates functions by trigger events. You will see logs for both in the same console.*

We should also make sure the trigger is happening on the appropriate write. We want to be able to track all writes to the alerts table. To do this, we need to reference only `alerts/{pushId}`. If we wanted to only look at writes specifically related to room numbers, we could do this by referencing `alerts/{pushId}/roomnumber`. This is something that is good to keep in mind for future iterations. You could have several functions that all read on different keys in the alerts JSON tree.

Reacting to the Triggered Event

We want to continue building out our application by creating the functionality of the storage triggered function. Right now, we have two needs for this function:

1. Send a text to the guest to let them know their request has been received and a service is on its way.

2. Update the database to reflect this change and let the function know the alert has been sent out.

To handle the text message requirement, we will go back to our Twilio account and utilize this service for text messaging. If you didn't set up a Twilio account for the Azure chapter, please go back and take care of that now. We are going to use Firebase environment variables to store the auth token and the account ID. The Firebase SDK for Cloud Functions offers built in environment configuration to make it easy to store and retrieve secure data for our project without having to redeploy.

To store our Twilio data, we can use the following Firebase command in our Command Line:

```
firebase functions:config:set twilioservice.authtoken="XXXXXXXXXXXXX" twilioservice.
accountsid="XXXXXXXXXXXX"
```

To check that our information was stored correctly, we can access the environment variables by using the following Firebase command:

```
firebase functions:config:get
```

The following demonstrates what this process should look like in your terminal:

```
mbp-mstigler:HTTPTrigger mstigler$ firebase functions:config:set twilioservice.authtoken="
XXXXXXXXXXXX " twilioservice.accountsid=" XXXXXXXXXXXX "
✔ Functions config updated.
```

Please deploy your functions for the change to take effect by running **firebase deploy --only
functions**

```
mbp-mstigler:HTTPTrigger mstigler$ firebase functions:config:get
{
 "twilioservice": {
  "accountsid": " XXXXXXXXXXXX ",
  "authtoken": " XXXXXXXXXXXX "
 }
}
```

Now we have set up our environment variables and can use them throughout our storage function. The following code establishes the Twilio client with our two authentication pieces, stores the incoming query strings as local variables, creates a message using these variables, and sends it to the recipient.

```
'use strict'

const functions = require('firebase-functions');
const admin = require('firebase-admin');

exports.handler = (event) => {
  const accountSid = functions.config().twilioservice.accountsid;
  const authToken = functions.config().twilioservice.authtoken;
  const client = require('twilio')(accountSid, authToken);

  var alert = event.data.val();
  console.log("Alert " + JSON.stringify(alert));
  var number = alert.phoneNumber;
  var name = alert.name;
  var room = alert.roomnumber;
  client.messages.create({
    from: '+18178544390',
    to: number,
    body: "Hello " + name + "! Your request is on the way to room " + room +"."
  }, function(err, message) {
    if(err) {
      console.error(err.message);
    }
  });

  return event.data.ref.parent.child('alertSent').set("alert has been sent");

};
```

We can test this code by deploying it and passing in a query string with the four required variables. If all goes well, you should receive a text from your Twilio trial account with the message body you provided (Figure 5-29).

Figure 5-29. *Postman accepts the same request and will accept a JSON body format*

Once we have the texting portion of this function complete, we can go ahead and add the logic to add to our Realtime database upon sent text message. To do this, we are going to add an `alertSent` field with a message that describes whether the alert has been sent.

```
return event.data.ref.parent.child('alertSent').set("alert has been sent");
```

We will write this `return` statement at the end of our storage JavaScript file. It sets an `alertSent` sibling in the Alerts database and returns a promise. We are setting a sibling so we can keep our alert data structure the same while still providing new information.

■ **Note**   When you perform asynchronous tasks inside Google Cloud functions with Firebase, they must return a *promise*. In this case, a promise includes writing to the Firebase Realtime Database. Setting a variable in the database returns a promise.

When we trigger it again, we should now see this new value in our Realtime database (Figure 5-30).

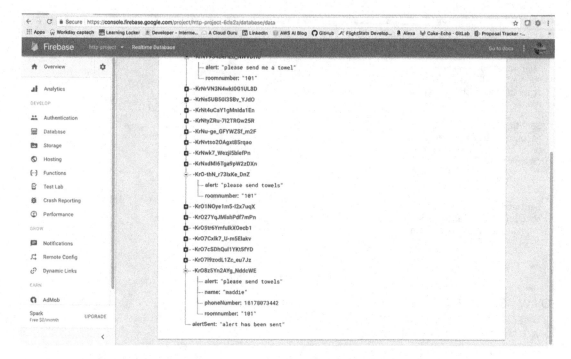

Figure 5-30. *Our Realtime database has now been updated to reflect the new sibling* alertSent

We can also check the status of our function through the logging capabilities of Firebase. If you navigate to the Functions tab, you will see a Logs tab at the top. This will show logs for all functions in the selected project. The logs will be sorted by time and will distinguish between a console.log statement, function success statements, and errors. You will also be able to see what function the logs are associated with.

In Figure 5-31 you can see I have incoming logs for both functions as one triggers another.

Figure 5-31. *Logging in Firebase is very similar to logging in Cloud Functions in the Google console*

You can also view these logs in the Google Cloud console when we use a Google Cloud project to import into Firebase. Overall, Firebase shares a lot of the same capabilities that the Google Cloud environment provides. It is good to get exposure to this because the two environments are very integrated and going forward I predict their being even more integrated.

In the next section, we are going to look at a pub/sub trigger in the Google Cloud console and learn how to take our Google Cloud projects and view them and execute them using Firebase.

IMPROVING OUR SERVERLESS FUNCTION

Improve by separating logic and utilizing serverless framework

Separate AWS logic from handler:

1. Use environment variables for AWS-specific logic or move AWS logic to a shared folder.

2. Create a Services folder that is specific to AWS and serves DynamoDB data.

Utilize the Serverless Framework:

1. Follow instructions for AWS setup on Serverless Framework.

2. Develop and deploy a function using Serverless Framework instead of manually.

The code for both of these improvements on the project can be found here: `https://github.com/mgstigler/Serverless/tree/master/AWS/aws-service/HTTPTrigger`.

In the next section, we will use the skills and tools we learned with the HTTP Trigger to create a separate Lambda function triggered by a storage event.

Pub/Sub Event

In this serverless function, we are going to create a function that is triggered by a Pub/Sub event. We will create this function in the Google Cloud console and will then import the project to Firebase to test it and view the logs.

What Is Google Cloud Pub/Sub?

Google Cloud Pub/Sub provides scalable, flexible, and reliable, message oriented middleware. It provides many-to-many asynchronous messaging that decouples senders and receivers. It offers highly available communication between independently written applications. Google provides several common scenarios that exemplify use cases for the Pub/Sub service. These scenarios include:

-   **Balancing workloads in network clusters:** A large queue of tasks can be efficiently distributed among multiple workers, such as Google Compute Engine instances.

-   **Implementing asynchronous workflows:** An order processing application can place an order on a topic, from which it can be processed by one or more workers.

-   **Distributing event notifications:** A service that accepts user signups can send notifications whenever a new user registers, and downstream services can subscribe to receive notifications of the event.

-   **Refreshing distributed caches:** An application can publish invalidation events to update the IDs of objects that have changed.

-   **Logging to multiple systems:** A Google Compute Engine instance can write logs to the monitoring system, to a database for later querying, and so on.

- **Data streaming from various processes or devices:** A residential sensor can stream data to backend servers hosted in the cloud.

- **Reliability improvement:** A single-zone Compute Engine service can operate in additional zones by subscribing to a common topic, to recover from failures in a zone or region.

The main concepts in Pub/Sub include the publisher, message, topic, subscription, and subscriber. Figure 5-32 illustrates how these components work together to create a unified message flow.

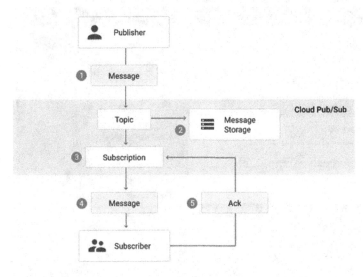

Figure 5-32. *The publisher creates a message that is posted to a topic with a series of subscriptions that all receive the message*

The following describes each of the resources used in the model. It is important to understand these concepts before jumping into the creation of our serverless function:

- **Topic:** A named resource to which messages are sent by publishers.

- **Subscription:** A named resource representing the stream of messages from a single, specific topic, to be delivered to the subscribing application.

- **Message:** The combination of data and (optional) attributes that a publisher sends to a topic and is eventually delivered to subscribers.

- **Message attribute:** A key-value pair that a publisher can define for a message.

Google Cloud has a concept of *background functions*, which operate differently than HTTP functions. We use background functions whenever we want our function to be invoked indirectly via a message on a Google Cloud Pub/Sub topic or a change in a Google Cloud Storage bucket. The background functions take two parameters, an event and an optional callback function.

Creating Our Pub/Sub Function

We are going to go ahead and create our Pub/Sub triggered function. First, we will need to create a Pub/Sub topic that we want to trigger our function. From the Google Cloud console, navigate to the Pub/Sub service and click Create a Topic (Figure 5-33). We are going to create a topic called AlertService. This will be the topic that triggers our function.

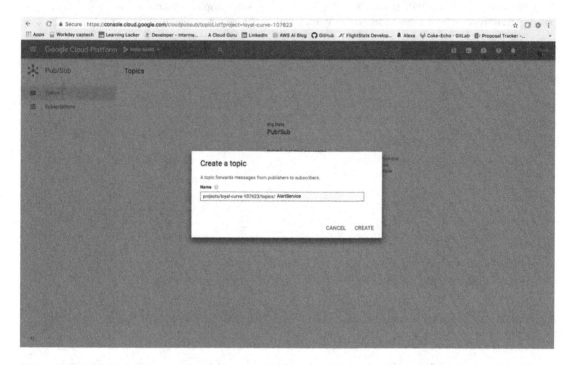

Figure 5-33. *Create a topic to trigger our function. Any posts to this topic will cause our function to execute.*

After we have created our topic, we are going to navigate back to the Google Cloud Functions panel and create a new function within our current project. We will make our trigger the Pub/Sub topic we just created. To test the functionality of using the Pub/Sub topic, we will initialize our function with the provided Google Cloud template. This simply writes the event to the logs.

```
/**
 * Triggered from a message on a Cloud Pub/Sub topic.
 *
 * @param {!Object} event The Cloud Functions event.
 * @param {!Function} The callback function.
 */
exports.subscribe = function subscribe(event, callback) {
 // The Cloud Pub/Sub Message object.
 const pubsubMessage = event.data;

 // We're just going to log the message to prove that
 // it worked.
 console.log(Buffer.from(pubsubMessage.data, 'base64').toString());
```

```
// Don't forget to call the callback.
 callback();
};
```

When we go back to our Pub/Sub topic, we can click Publish Message, write a message, and send it to our topic. If all goes as planned, we can view our message in our logs in Google Cloud. When you get a success response, import our project into our Firebase console. To do this, navigate to `console.firebase.google.com` and click Import Google Project. Import the overall project. Mine is still named Hello World.

You can then view the Pub/Sub function in the Functions tab. You should see the topic `AlertService` as the trigger and the execution that you just invoked. If you click on Logs, you will also see the logs for that Pub/Sub invocation we just created.

We are now going to add to our function so it does a little more than just logging to the console. Go ahead and do another `firebase init` in your project folder where your `index.js` file is stored. When prompted to select a project, select the Google Cloud project we have been developing in. Now, when we get a request through our topic, we want to store it in the `alerts` table in our Realtime database.

The following code demonstrates how we will handle the incoming request.

```
'use strict';
const functions = require('firebase-functions');
const admin = require('firebase-admin');
admin.initializeApp(functions.config().firebase);

exports.subscribe = functions.pubsub.topic('AlertService').onPublish(event => {
  const pubSubMessage = event.data;
  // Get the `name` attribute of the PubSub message JSON body.
  let alert = null;
  try {
   alert = pubSubMessage.json.alert;
   console.log("Alert: " + alert);
   admin.database().ref('/alerts').push({alert: alert}).then(snapshot => {
    console.log("success!");
   });

  } catch (e) {
   console.error('PubSub message was not JSON', e);
  }
});
```

Deploy this code using the `firebase deploy` command in your terminal. We can then test this functionality by going back to our Pub/Sub topic and sending a message. Our function is looking for a JSON body with an alert field. So the request will look like Figure 5-34.

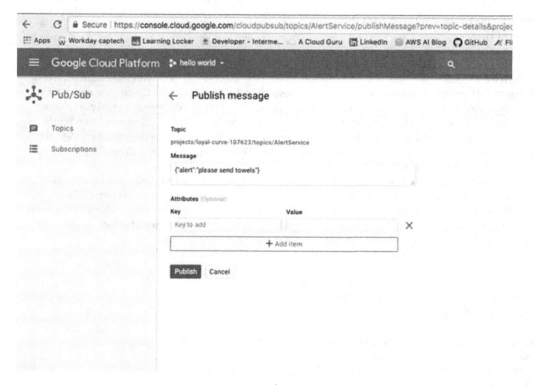

Figure 5-34. *Send a message to our topic to trigger our recently deployed function*

You should be able to track the progress of the function by looking at the logs in the Firebase environment. You can also track this in the Google Cloud functions environment. Our function was renamed to subscribe and you can see its invocations under Function Details (Figure 5-35). Upon success, the alert that we sent along the Pub/Sub will appear under alerts/ in our Realtime database.

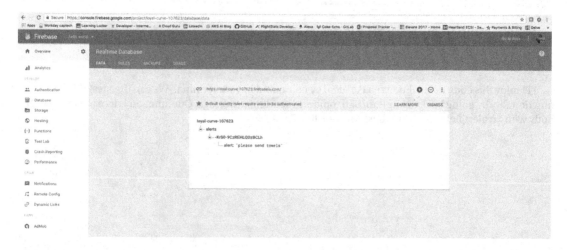

Figure 5-35. *Our message is now stored in our project's Realtime database*

We now have a function that is hosted in Google Cloud and also accessed by Firebase. You can view logging and triggers in both environments and can easily update and deploy the function so it is accessible by both consoles. The purpose of this exercise was to show this communication between functions and to show how to access Cloud triggers and have them affect a Firebase database.

IMPROVING OUR SERVERLESS FUNCTION

Improve by integrating with our previous application

Add the Pub/Sub function to our original `index.js` file associated with Firebase.

1. Use the same logic we used for our storage trigger and add our Pub/Sub function to the `index.js` in our HTTP function to be deployed together.

2. This will keep all of our functions together as one application.

Deploy the project as a Google Cloud project.

3. Host all of the projects under Google Cloud and import the entire project to Firebase instead of having them stored separately.

Conclusion

In this chapter we explored several serverless applications with Google Cloud functions. We saw differences between Google Cloud and AWS and Azure. We also learned the basics of Google Cloud including navigating the console, configuring functions, establishing triggers such as HTTP and background triggers, as well as some other popular integrated services like Firebase. At this point, you have experience building functions with three different cloud providers. You should be able to differentiate between the providers and have a better understanding of the pros and cons of each. We have also explored several ways to apply serverless architecture. Some applications were more personal and others served actual business cases.

The code for this section can also be found on the GitHub site at:

```
https://github.com/mgstigler/Serverless/tree/master/GoogleCloud
```

In the next chapter, we will explore cloud-agnostic solutions to serverless applications. We will use knowledge from the previous chapters to create this solution.

CHAPTER 6

■ ■ ■

An Agnostic Approach

At this point, we have explored serverless architectures using the three cloud providers: Amazon Web Services, Microsoft Azure, and Google Cloud. We have created applications that use HTTP triggers and storage triggers and respond to them by making changes in the provider-specific services. Through these exercises, we have seen many use cases for these types of applications and provider-specific use cases. In this chapter, we will take a step back and look at how to create solutions that aren't dependent on the specific provider. We will explore use cases and examples of application architectures that remove the provider specific logic from the functions and leverage the universality of serverless code to provide completely agnostic solutions.

■ **Note**   You will need a basic understanding of how each of the provider's services work in order to complete the exercises in this chapter. If you have not gone through the examples for the three providers, please do so.

In this chapter, we will spend some time discussing the need for agnostic solutions, what that means for future serverless applications, the approach that we will use to present a solution, the code we will use to create the solution, and a serverless example using a database trigger.

Need for Agnostic Solutions

Before we begin developing an agnostic solution, I think it is important to identify why this is such an important concept to tackle and why it is even worth approaching. I'm going to start by identifying a current case study I have developed for my client, a global insurance company.

The Current State

My client is a world leader in the travel insurance and assistance industry. They help people anytime, anywhere to find solutions to any travel-related problem. Their partners number in the thousands and include travel agencies, airlines, resorts, websites, event ticket brokers, corporations, universities, and credit card companies.

This company is owned by the world's largest diversified insurance company. Thanks, in large part, to the scale of its parent company, it is able to provide innovative products with worldwide coverage at a competitive rate.

Over 25 million travelers depend on this company every year to protect them while they're away from home. It provides a wide range of assistance and concierge services that can help its customers get the most out of their trip. The company has been helping protect the fabric of America for more than 100 years. In fact, this client insured the Wright Brothers' first flight, the construction of the Golden Gate Bridge, and many Hollywood movies.

© Maddie Stigler 2018
M. Stigler, *Beginning Serverless Computing*, https://doi.org/10.1007/978-1-4842-3084-8_6

With this reputation and amount of services and clients involved, this client places a lot of importance on its technical stack and architecture. With the current state, the company is currently involved with one cloud provider but most of its infrastructure is in-house. Management wants to move the entire infrastructure to the cloud, but with so many dependencies and a headquarters abroad, that is obviously easier said than done.

The company's first step toward the transition to the cloud has involved a starter application that automates claim payments for trip delays and cancellations. The proposed architecture for this solution involves several AWS Lambda functions and many services in AWS. There are four major parts to this execution that are detailed in Figure 6-1.

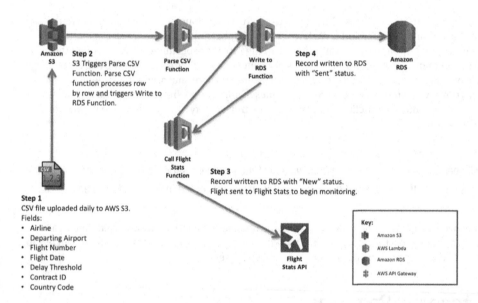

Figure 6-1. *The CSV load flow demonstrates the transfer of data from on-premises to the AWS Lambda functions*

The current architecture with this cloud solution involves communicating between an on-premises database and an AWS database. The on-premises site still stores all of the customer and flight data that is needed to make this application work. On top of this, the changes required to make this transition are not simple changes. They are company-wide changes that require a lot of time, resources, and process training. Even providing a simple CSV file requires approval by headquarters, security, and the entire IT department. This is very standard across industries.

Figure 6-2 shows the notification workflow, which takes an incoming flightstats request (such as a delay or a cancellation).

Notify Workflow

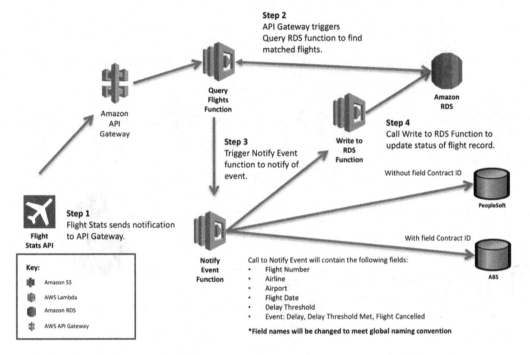

Step 2
API Gateway triggers
Query RDS function to find
matched flights.

Query
Flights
Function

Amazon
API
Gateway

Amazon
RDS

Step 4
Call Write to RDS Function to
update status of flight record.

Step 3
Trigger Notify Event
function to notify of
event.

Write to
RDS
Function

Without field Contract ID

PeopleSoft

Step 1
Flight Stats sends notification
to API Gateway.

With field Contract ID

Flight
Stats API

ABS

Notify
Event
Function

Call to Notify Event will contain the following fields:
• Flight Number
• Airline
• Airport
• Flight Date
• Delay Threshold
• Event: Delay, Delay Threshold Met, Flight Cancelled

Key:

![Amazon S3] Amazon S3

![AWS Lambda] AWS Lambda

![Amazon RDS] Amazon RDS

![AWS API Gateway] AWS API Gateway

*Field names will be changed to meet global naming convention

Figure 6-2. The Notify workflow demonstrates the flow of data from the FlightStats API back to the Lambda
functions that handle the flight data

The Notify workflow, similar to the CSV flow, relies on communication with the on-premises database
to be successful. It also relies on a data transfer and update in Amazon RDS to send the appropriate data
back to the on-premises database.

Figure 6-3 demonstrates the SMS workflow, which takes a number and a text message from the
on-premises database and sends a text to the customer.

SMS Flow

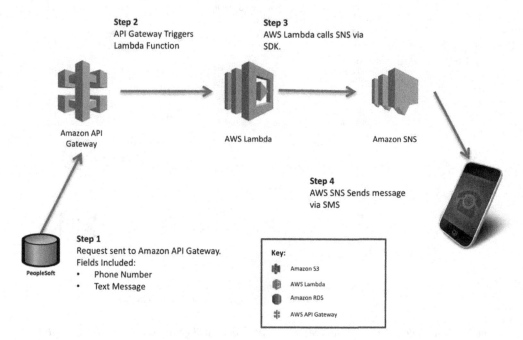

Step 2
API Gateway Triggers
Lambda Function

Step 3
AWS Lambda calls SNS via
SDK.

Amazon API
Gateway

AWS Lambda

Amazon SNS

Step 4
AWS SNS Sends message
via SMS

PeopleSoft

Step 1
Request sent to Amazon API Gateway.
Fields Included:
• Phone Number
• Text Message

Key:

Amazon S3

AWS Lambda

Amazon RDS

AWS API Gateway

Figure 6-3. *The SMS flow demonstrates the ability of the application to notify customers when a flight has been delayed or cancelled to the extent that a claim can be filed automatically*

Once again the flow depends on internal data flowing in and out to be able to text the customer with their flight delay and cancellation information. The next flow updates the table information in the on-premises database to be cleared every two weeks. This is triggered by a cloud watch timer that executes a Lambda function that reaches out to the on-premises system to clear out the old and outdated flight data. Figure 6-4 demonstrates this process.

Update Tables Flow

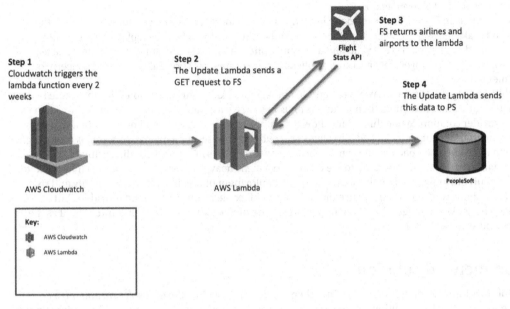

Figure 6-4. The Update Tables flow demonstrates the Lambda function flow that updates the cloud database as well as the on-premises database

The bottom line with all of these flows and processes within the new architecture is that they depend on both the on-premises infrastructure and the AWS infrastructure. While it is a very well designed system and a great idea from a customer standpoint, there are many concerns from a business and overall architecture standpoint.

Business Problems

Given the provided architecture and flow diagrams, there are several business problems that have been raised. One of the major problems is the dependence on AWS Lambda functions. One of the proposed solutions is to host the application on EC2 instances, where the environment could be controlled and dockerized. However, this solution also involves writing all of the SNS components independently of the services because we would want to be completely removed from the AWS environments.

The client is currently dependent on one cloud provider for part of its services but does not want to be entirely dependent on this provider, nor does it want to be partially dependent on many cloud providers. A fear with going with AWS is the dependence on this provider overall. And while the client is planning on shifting its entire infrastructure to AWS, management still holds the very rational fear of being locked into AWS as a vendor.

In my opinion there are several reasons behind this fear of vendor lock-in. One is the need to avoid a long re-engineering effort if the client ever decides to change providers. This makes sense because it is something companies are dealing with on a daily basis. And if we take it back a level, companies switching from on-premises services to cloud services are already making a huge move that requires a lot of effort and a lot of process engineering. On top of that, they face the fear of switching providers, which requires the same amount of effort all over again.

Another reason for this fear rests in the idea that a single cloud computing vendor will overtake the market and make it less of a choice. In this case, the only solution would be to redeploy and architect for a different vendor. This fear is very valid and a common one among large and small companies. The fear of losing all of your employee data and core application functionality is very real and a good concern for companies to have.

While my client was sold on AWS as a vendor, management knew this was a potential end-game for the cloud solution and presented their concerns to us in a very reasonable manner. One option was to have a cross-provider solution. While this would allow the company to use services and products in a cross-provider environment, it is still locked into whatever vendor it chooses for whatever service it is providing.

From a business perspective, the vendor lock-in concern is a serious one. In addition, the transformation of large historical data to the cloud also weighs heavy on businesses. The cost may be better in the long run but looking at it in the short and quick deployment phase, it tends to seem costly and risky.

The company wants to be able to use the scalable and flexible resources of cloud providers, but struggles with making changes that could impact the future of the company's infrastructure as well as the responsiveness toward its clientele.

Recommended Solution

To be able to address all of the concerns of the client while still providing the best solution and most cost-effective solution, the best solution would be to develop an application that is provider-independent. In this situation, the company still gets all of the rewards of relying on a cloud provider without wreaking any of the potential downfalls of falling into vendor lock-in.

The tricky part of this is implementing the solution correctly. We have already seen scenarios in which we remove cloud logic from the functionality. This would build from that idea and remove the cloud provider logic entirely and provide it in many forms.

For instance, we would have one solution that could switch between AWS, Azure, and Google Cloud simultaneously. Figure 6-5 shows a rough execution of this solution with the first step in the updated overall CSV load flow.

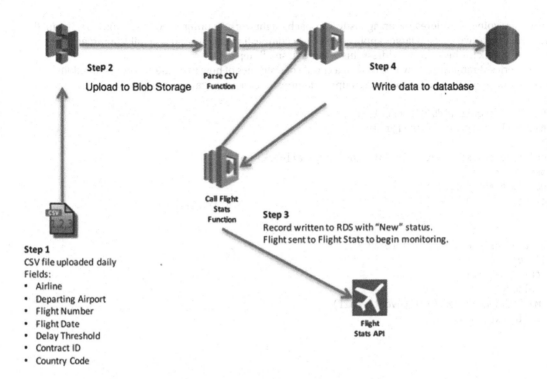

Step 2

Upload to Blob Storage

Parse CSV Function

Step 4

Write data to database

Call Flight Stats Function

Step 3
Record written to RDS with "New" status.
Flight sent to Flight Stats to begin monitoring.

Flight Stats API

Step 1
CSV file uploaded daily
Fields:
- Airline
- Departing Airport
- Flight Number
- Flight Date
- Delay Threshold
- Contract ID
- Country Code

Figure 6-5. *The solution is implemented without any knowledge of who the provider is*

In this flow, we create the same interaction that would happen during the CSV flow, except that the provider is not a part of it. This would be appealing to many businesses because they would be able to implement cloud solutions without fear of vendor lock-in, and yet also with fear of vendor lock-in.

The way this solution works, you would be able to exist as a company with vendor lock-in and then switch vendors as necessary. For our recommended solution, we will look into a solution that relies on this vendor lock-in yet knows it's a weakness enough to code directly for this weakness.

Define the Approach

While we can identify the obvious business need for an agnostic approach, it is also appropriate to assess this situation on an application-by-application approach. For instance, I might be developing an Alexa Skills application that I want to be accessible by only Amazon Lambda functions. In other occurrences, for instance with the client situation, I would want it to be accessible by all client functions. Or, suppose I wanted my code for my Alexa Skill to translate to Google Home, Apple's Siri, or Microsoft's Cortana. These are very reasonable needs. Companies want their products to be accessible across platforms and products to reach a wider audience.

The serverless architecture makes this jump more feasible than you would think. If we were to try to apply this logic within virtual machines or applications with infrastructure, we would have a harder time. We would be required to set up entirely different services within these environments and make them publicly accessible.

When you think about the different use cases for the agnostic approach, you can see how the code itself with its underlying logic shouldn't have to change. The only thing that separates these application environments is the environments themselves.

We are going to explore how an agnostic approach might work. In order to do this, I want to start small and then grow as we develop larger applications. To accomplish a scalable and accessible approach to this problem, I think the best way to address this is through small steps.

Serverless Framework provides us with a couple of examples of how to create serverless functions correctly and agnostically. The following snippet demonstrates a poor example of agnostic code.

```
const db = require('db').connect();
const mailer = require('mailer');

module.exports.saveUser = (event, context, callback) => {
 const user = {
  email: event.email,
  created_at: Date.now()
 }

 db.saveUser(user, function (err) {
  if (err) {
   callback(err);
  } else {
   mailer.sendWelcomeEmail(event.email);
   callback();
  }
 });
};
```

This code is a poor example for a couple of reasons:

- The business logic is not separate from the FaaS provider. It's bounded to the way AWS Lambda passes incoming data (Lambda's event object).

- Testing this function will rely on separate services. Specifically, running a database instance and a mail server.

How can we refactor this and make it executable yet not dependent on functions specific to AWS? The following code demonstrates how we can separate the logic from the execution.

```
class Users {
 constructor(db, mailer) {
  this.db = db;
  this.mailer = mailer;
 }

 save(email, callback) {
  const user = {
   email: email,
   created_at: Date.now()
  }
```

```
  this.db.saveUser(user, function (err) {
   if (err) {
    callback(err);
   } else {
    this.mailer.sendWelcomeEmail(email);
    callback();
   }
 });
 }
}

module.exports = Users;
```

This users class handles the incoming requests rather agnostically. The database and mailer are both provided externally. In this case, we could provide the class with an Azure db and mailer instance, a Google db and mailer instance, or an AWS db and mailer instance.

The following code demonstrates the index module that calls the Users class.

```
const db = require('db').connect();
const mailer = require('mailer');
const Users = require('users');

let users = new Users(db, mailer);

module.exports.saveUser = (event, context, callback) => {
 users.save(event.email, callback);
};
```

Now, the class we've defined here keeps business logic separate. Further, the code responsible for setting up dependencies, injecting them, calling business logic functions, and interacting with AWS Lambda is in its own file, which will be changed less often. This way, the business logic is not provider-dependent, and it's easier to re-use and to test.

Further, this code doesn't require running any external services. Instead of a real db and mailer services, we can pass mocks and assert if saveUser and sendWelcomeEmail have been called with proper arguments.

Unit tests can easily be written to cover this class. An integration test can be added by invoking the function (serverless invoke) with fixture email address It would then check whether the user is actually saved to DB and whether email was received to see if everything is working together.

Our approach to solving the agnostic scenario will follow a similar path. The index file or the main file executing the code will be blind to the provider and the logic and services associated with that provider. Figure 6-6 illustrates the feasibility of this approach.

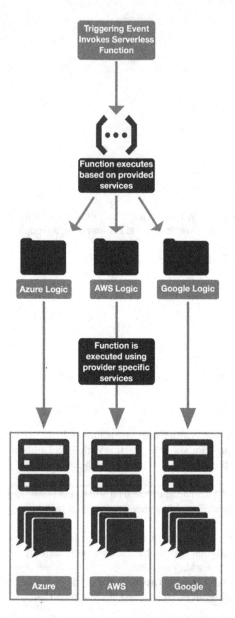

Figure 6-6. *The proposed solution keeps provider logic separate from the normal operation of the application. When the function is deployed, we select the provider we want to deploy with and use only its logic and services.*

With this proposed solution, the provider-specific code is kept separate from the index file. When it is time to deploy, you can select the appropriate provider logic code and deploy to that provider's environment. To make this even simpler, we will utilize the Serverless Framework to deploy the code.

The serverless.yml file includes a provider input field. We would need to change that depending on the provider and deploy making sure the triggers and services are all stated correctly per provider inside of this file. We could even have a serverless file for each provider and then chose which to deploy when we settle on a provider. The following code shows us where we can change the deployment provider when we need to:

```
# serverless.yml


service: azfx-node-http


provider:

  name: azure

  location: West US


plugins:

  - serverless-azure-functions


functions:

  hello:

    handler: handler.hello

    events:

      - http: true

        x-azure-settings:

          authLevel : anonymous
```

Now that we have a better understanding of our design approach, we can explore the Hello World code we will use to test the proof of concept at scale. We will stick with the three providers we have been using (Amazon, Azure, and Google) and will deploy with each provider and ensure that the function works the same.

Explore the Code

We will create a general project structure for our agnostic solution based on the proof-of-concept approach detailed previously. The first thing we will do is create a project structure in which the index file is at the root of the folder and there is a storage folder that contains separate AWS, Google, and Azure folders (Figure 6-7).

Figure 6-7. *The project structure stores cloud-provider–specific knowledge in different folders. This keeps it separate from the index file as well as from being confused with other provider logic.*

For our first demonstration of our proof of concept, we are simply going to make our index file log the provider environment it is in. We are also going to use Serverless Framework to deploy to different environments. We will begin by looking at our index file.

```
// dependencies
var provider = 'aws';
var Provider = require('./storage/' + provider + '/provider')

exports.handler = function (event, context, callback) {
  Provider.printProvider("Hello World");
}
```

The index file will have one value that you will have to update between deployments, and that is the provider variable. We will test the ability to easily switch between providers and pass index variables into different environments. Within each provider folder, we will add a provider JavaScript file.

The following code demonstrates what I have in my provider file. You will need to change the response per provider file.

```
// dependencies

module.exports = {
  printProvider: function(message) {
    console.log('Message: ' + message + ' from AWS!');
  }
}
```

The provider.printProvider function simply logs the message being passed from the index file with the provider's environment. We will also want to initialize a serverless.yml file within each provider's folder. Each serverless file will be specific to the provider.

The following code demonstrates an AWS serverless.yml file.

```
service: aws-nodejs

package:
 individually: true
 exclude:
  - ./**

provider:
 name: aws

functions:
 helloworld:
  handler: index.handler
  package:
   include:
    - ../../index.js
    - ../../storage/aws/**
    - node_modules/**
```

To switch the provider, simply change aws to azure or google. You will also need to update the package paths to reflect the correct path for the provider's logic. In this case, we would just be changing the folder path after ../../storage/.

Finally, we are ready to deploy our functions in their respective environments. To do this, simply navigate to the provider directory you want to deploy from and enter the following command into your terminal:

```
serverless deploy
```

This will deploy the suggested function into the correct provider environment. Do this with all three providers. Once they have all been deployed, we can log in to the individual consoles and see the effect of our changes.

■ **Note** I realize this feels like a very repetitive task with a lot of overhead, but keep in mind that in the real world, you would probably not be consistently deploying your applications in different environments. Instead you would be deploying them when you need them and when you are ready to switch providers.

We didn't establish a trigger for our serverless function, because we really just wanted to test the project structure as it is, as a proof of concept. So in order to test our function, in each environment you can trigger it with any request. If our implementation of our concept was successful, you will see the correct response message with the correct provider in the logs (Figure 6-8).

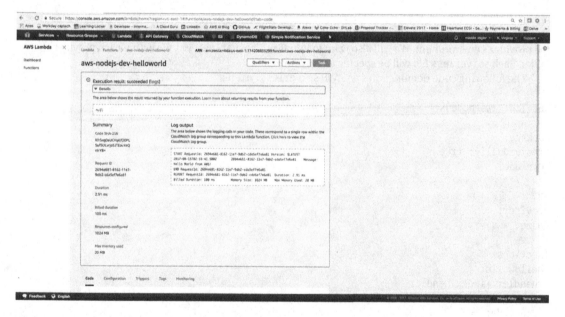

Figure 6-8. *Our proof of concept was successful. We can see the message from AWS clearly in the logs.*

We should be able to see this message change dynamically depending on the environment we deploy it to. One potential future development to keep in mind for this proof of concept is determining how to detect our environment and pull from the correct project folder once we realize what provider we are using.

That capability would be helpful for a couple of reasons. The first is that we would eliminate the manual process involved in switching the provider in the code. Some innovative groups have already started making moves in this direction. You can see this with Serverless Framework, which tries to make it as painless as possible to get your code deployed to whatever cloud provider you want.

However, even Serverless Framework requires you do setup to preface the deployment. This setup usually consists of specifying the cloud provider and initializing your CLI environment with this provider. That's not much compared to the manual process of deploying a project to functions, but I do think it is something that will be made even more seamless in the future. Cloud providers might even start making themselves more accessible and integral between different environments.

Just to confirm that this solution did work across multiple environments, I also tested the function in the Google and Azure platforms. As shown in Figure 6-9, both were successful and displayed the expected log statement.

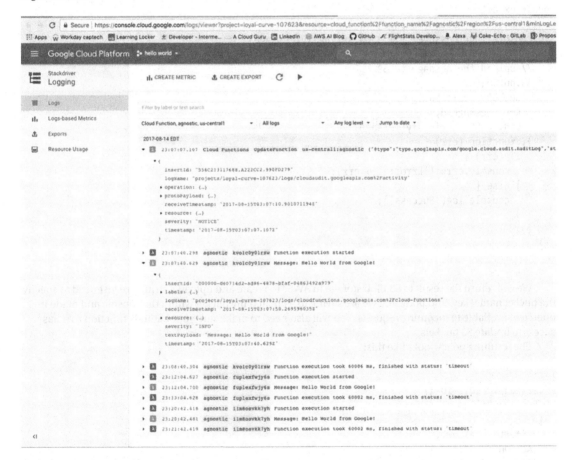

Figure 6-9. *The correct response message from Google Cloud Functions proves that not only does the Hello World function make successful requests, it is flexible and scalable across platforms*

Now that we have shown our proof of concept is functional across providers, we need to add actual cloud provider logic to it to prove that our concept is scalable. In the next section we will build upon this to add a storage component.

Code and Example Using the Database

To prove that our concept scales appropriately with different cloud logic, we are going to create an application that is triggered by an HTTP event and stores the event information of that trigger in Blob storage. We will continue using our Google Cloud scenario of a hotel room with a guest for our incoming data.

The first thing we want to do is add a storage JavaScript file in each of our provider's storage folders. This file is going to contain a function that takes in two parameters, a message and a message ID, and will store the message in the provider's Blob storage under the message ID value.

We can now write the code specific to the cloud provider for this logic.

```
// dependencies
var AWS = require('aws-sdk');
var S3 = new AWS.S3();
var BucketName = 'poc-cloudagnostic-maddie';

module.exports = {
  saveObject: function(message, messageId) {
    console.log('Message: ' + JSON.stringify(message));

    // upload the message to S3
    S3.putObject({
      Bucket: BucketName,
      Key: messageId,
      Body: JSON.stringify(message)
    }, function (err) {
      if (err) {
        console.error('Error: ' + err);
      } else {
        console.log('Success');
      }
    });
  }
}
```

We will return the result to S3 Blob storage in AWS. To create and upload a string, we just need to specify the bucket name, key, and body that we are saving to. I created my bucket within the console and made it open and available to incoming requests. You will also need to make sure your Lambda function role has access to update S3 buckets.

The resulting policy looks like this:

```
{
 "Version": "2012-10-17",
 "Statement": [
  {
   "Effect": "Allow",
   "Action": "s3:*",
   "Resource": "*"
  }
 ]
}
```

We also want to create our storage service for Azure. Like AWS, Azure also requires a Blob storage name for the bucket, the message you want stored, and the message ID you want your message stored under. As you can see, the code is very similar between these two providers. We could probably extract even more of it and make it even dumber.

```
// dependencies
var azure = require('azure-storage');
var blobClient = azure.createBlobService();
var containerName = 'poc-cloudagnostic';

module.exports = {
  saveObject: function(message, messageId) {
    console.log('Message: ' + message);
    message = JSON.stringify(message);
    blobClient.createBlockBlobFromText(containerName, messageId, message, function(error,
    result, response) {
      if(error) {
        console.log("Couldn't upload");
        console.error(error);
      } else {
        console.log("Upload successful!");
      }
    })
  }
}
```

For Google Cloud storage, we once again have a code structure very similar to the previous cloud providers. The main difference here is that we need to specify the projectId and the keyFilename that the function is under. The project ID is the unique ID that Google assigns your project at setup. You can grab it from your dashboard.

The keyFilename is simply looking for the path to your keyfile.json document. To locate this, pull up your Cloud Shell through your console and enter this command:

```
pwd keyfile.json
```

It should be stored somewhere in the home/user/ directory. After that connection is established, we just need to create a bucket and upload our event to the bucket.

```
// dependencies
var storage = require('@google-cloud/storage');
var gcs = storage({
  projectId: 'loyal-curve-107623',
  keyFilename: '/home/maddie_stigler'
});
var containerName = 'poc-cloudagnostic';

module.exports = {
  saveObject: function(message, messageId) {
    console.log('Message: ' + message);
    gcs.createBucket(containerName, function(err, bucket) {
      //bucket created
```

```
    if(!err) {
      var bucket = gcs.bucket(containerName);
      bucket.upload(JSON.stringify(message), function(err, file) {
        if(!err) {
          console.log("success");
        }
      })
    }
  });

}
}
```

As you can see, a lot of the storage execution in our cloud provider functions is very similar. We could probably convert a lot of this code to use environment variables so that we don't replicate it across projects. For now, we will leave it as is to test and make sure everything is still functioning properly.

The next piece of code we need to update is the index.handler module. As in the Provider module, we will require the Storage module and call it in the body by sending it the incoming event and a string for the keyfilename. I am just going to use 1 for now.

```
// dependencies
var provider = 'aws';
var Provider = require('./storage/' + provider + '/provider');
var Storage = require('./storage/' + provider + '/storage');

exports.handler = function (event, context, callback) {
  console.info(event);
  Provider.printProvider("Hello World");
  Storage.saveObject(event, '1');
}
```

The last thing we need to do before moving on and testing our code is to update our serverless. yml file. We need to be sure that our storage.json file is being included in the project zip. We also need to configure the HTTP trigger.

```
helloWorld:
  handler: index.handler
  events:
   - http:
     method: post
  package:
      include:
   - ../../index.js
   - ../../storage/aws/**
   - node_modules/**
```

If you wanted to include a path for your HTTP event as we did in some previous examples, you could also configure that in the serverless file. I recommend going to https://serverless.com/framework/docs/ and reading the documentation for the particular cloud provider you are looking at.

Now we are ready to deploy. We can follow the same procedure that we followed earlier by using serverless deployment in each project folder. Once they are all deployed, we can go into the console and set up a test event to try and trigger our function.

I am going to show examples from just AWS, but these functions should be working for all cloud provider environments.

The POST request I'm going to send in is this:

```
{
    "name": "Maddie",
    "roomnumber": "117"
}
```

When we test in the AWS portal, we get a success message with the logging statements we included (Figure 6-10).

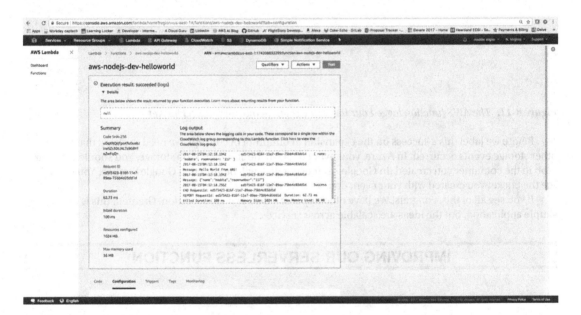

Figure 6-10. *The AWS function returns a successful response in the console test event*

We now need to make sure our event made it to S3. Navigate to the bucket you created. You should see a new 1 object stored in it (Figure 6-11). If you did, congrats! If not, go back and check on your code and make sure everything is defined correctly.

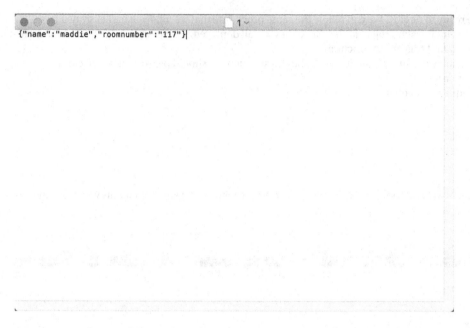

Figure 6-11. *The AWS function logged our incoming event to our specified S3 bucket*

Before we label this a success on the expansion of our proof of concept, we need to check that the two other storage events occurred. In Azure, your event data will be stored in Blob storage. You should see your Blob in the container you created. In Google, your event data will be stored in Google Storage. You should see the bucket you created with your event data stored in it.

If you see all of this, congrats! We have officially created an agnostic solution. Granted, this is a very simple application, but the ideas are scalable across services.

IMPROVING OUR SERVERLESS FUNCTION

Improve by using environment variables and enforcing models

Use environment variables to store the variables we are repeating in our provider logic:

- Use Environment variables either in Serverless Framework or stored directly in the provider's environment:

```
#  Define function environment variables here
#  environment:
#    variable2: value2
```

Environment variables will keep our buckets and paths consistent across providers. They will also ensure that we don't repeat code too often across provider logic.

Use models to enforce incoming requests:

1. Set up authorization on our endpoint and make sure these authorization keys are stored properly either as environment variables or in the provider console.

2. Use JavaScript models to structure the incoming data:

```
export interface requestModel {
  name: string,
  roomnumber: string
}
```

3. We can also implement request method checks as we did in the Google Cloud example.

The code for both of these improvements on the project can be found here: `https://github.com/mgstigler/Serverless/tree/master/CloudAgnostic/`

Conclusion

In this final chapter, we explore ways to make our code cloud-agnostic. In this sense, we were able to access AWS, Azure, and Google Cloud services within one function. If the business owner ever decided to settle on one cloud provider over another, that would be covered under this solution. You learned how to integrate different cloud services into different cloud functions and have them easily accessible within their own environments. At this point, you should be able to distinguish between which provider's functions are being triggered and how are they are handling them in this state. This chapter is important because it addresses concerns of real clients and proposes a solution to the issue.

The code for this chapter can also be found on the GitHub site at:

`https://github.com/mgstigler/Serverless/tree/master`

This might be the end of the novel, but I will continue adding to each chapter as the knowledge for each one expands beyond what I originally thought.

Index

Get the eBook for only $5!

Why limit yourself?

With most of our titles available in both PDF and ePUB format, you can access your content wherever and however you wish—on your PC, phone, tablet, or reader.

Since you've purchased this print book, we are happy to offer you the eBook for just $5.

To learn more, go to http://www.apress.com/companion or contact support@apress.com.

Apress®

Printed in the United States
By Bookmasters